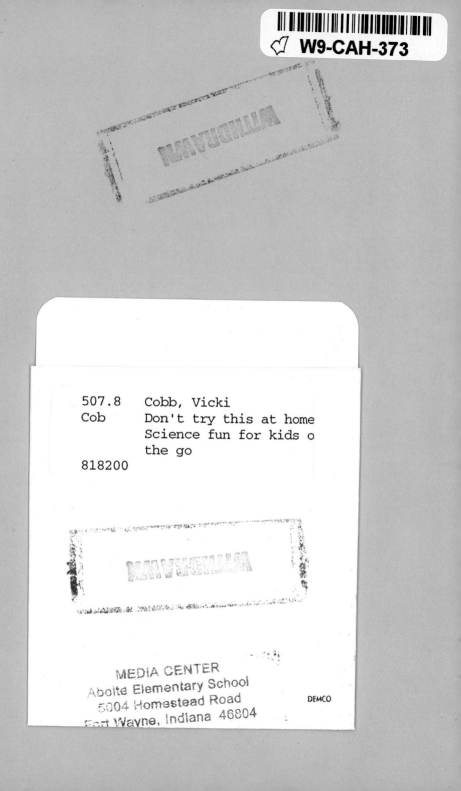

# Don't Try This at Home!

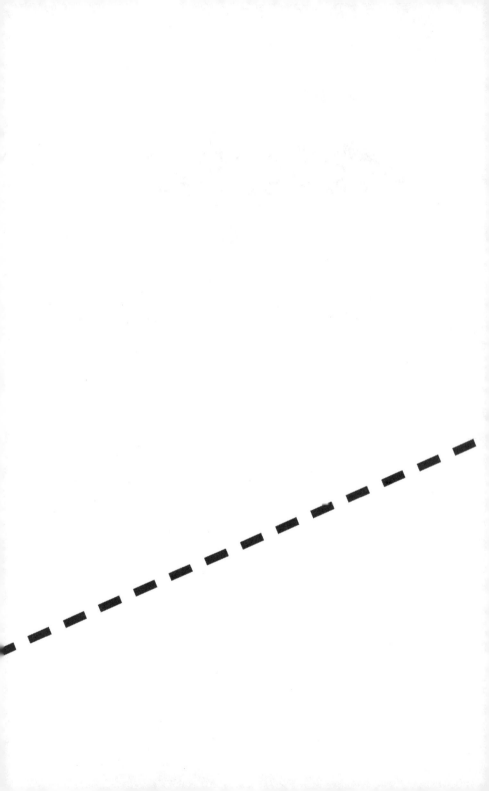

## More Science Fun

*by* **VICKI COBB** *and* **KATHY DARLING**

**Bet You Can't**
*Science Impossibilities to Fool You*

**Bet You Can!**
*Science Possibilities to Fool You*

**Wanna Bet?**
*Science Challenges to Fool You*

# Don't Try This at Home!

## at Home!

### Science Fun
### for Kids on the Go

VICKI COBB
and KATHY DARLING
illustrated by TRUE KELLEY

MORROW JUNIOR BOOKS
*New York*

MEDIA CENTER
Aboite Elementary School
5004 Homestead Road
Fort Wayne, Indiana 46804

*This book is dedicated to*
*FERDINAND MAGELLAN.*
*When he left home, he went a long, long way.*

**Please note that some of the experiments in this book are to be performed under adult supervision.**

Text copyright © 1998 by Vicki Cobb and Kathy Darling
Illustrations copyright © 1998 by True Kelley

Published by Morrow Junior Books
a division of William Morrow and Company, Inc.
1350 Avenue of the Americas, New York, NY 10019
www.williammorrow.com

Printed in the United States of America.

1   2   3   4   5   6   7   8   9   10

Library of Congress Cataloging-in-Publication Data
Cobb, Vicki.
Don't try this at home!: science fun for kids on the go/
by Vicki Cobb and Kathy Darling.
p.  cm.
Summary: Provides instructions for a variety of science activities outside, arranged by such categories as school, parks, and vehicles.
ISBN 0-688-14856-5
1. Science—Experiments—Juvenile literature.   2. Science—Study and teaching— Activity programs—Juvenile literature.   3. Scientific recreations—Juvenile literature.   [1. Science—Experiments.   2. Experiments.   3. Scientific recreations.]
I. Darling, Kathy.   II. Title.
Q164.C483  1998    507.8—dc21    97-20481    CIP  AC

# Contents

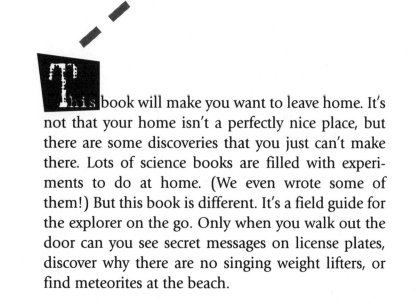

# The Right Place
## at the Right Time

**T**his book will make you want to leave home. It's not that your home isn't a perfectly nice place, but there are some discoveries that you just can't make there. Lots of science books are filled with experiments to do at home. (We even wrote some of them!) But this book is different. It's a field guide for the explorer on the go. Only when you walk out the door can you see secret messages on license plates, discover why there are no singing weight lifters, or find meteorites at the beach.

Some people may think you're a bit strange if they see you balancing on soda cans or blowing bubbles when the temperature is below zero. Don't let anyone discourage you. You're just being curious, a natural human trait. After all, Benjamin Franklin flew a kite in a thunderstorm and look what he discovered—electricity!

All you need is an inquisitive mind and an adventurous spirit. We've supplied clear instructions on how to do dozens and dozens of amazing activities, plus insider information that will let you fascinate friends, impress parents—even teach your teachers. If knowledge is power, you can be a mighty source.

Wherever you go, whatever you do, check this book first. It's organized by place. The chapter headings in the table of contents give a general idea of where you have to be to do the activities. There is also a special index in the back of the book that lists activities by specific location and keys them to special conditions, such as the time of day or season of the year. Some of the experiments in the book require extra care for safety. Make sure you have an adult assistant when you do them.

The world is filled with opportunities for discovery. Most people miss them, but you won't. You'll be in the right place at the right time—with the right information—if you've got this book with you!

# Outside–The Realm of Possibility

# SPY LICENSE

*Where:* Driveways, parking lots
*Special Conditions:* Night or day

## Doing the Deed

Counterfeit license plates are used by car thieves. The counterfeits may look authentic to ordinary people, but police know how to detect the fakes. You can too, but you need to look at license plates from a whole new angle. Many license plates have secret images—but it's the viewing angle that reveals them. Although different states have different identifying symbols, they are almost always placed in a vertical row down the center of the plate.

The secret symbols are invisible unless you view the plate from an angle of thirty degrees. So stand facing the license plate at a distance of four to eight feet. The correct distance for you depends on your height. The taller you are, the farther away you'll have to stand.

We easily saw the outline of New York State on our license plates in the daytime. But it was even more dramatic at night when the image was illuminated by a flashlight held near our eyes.

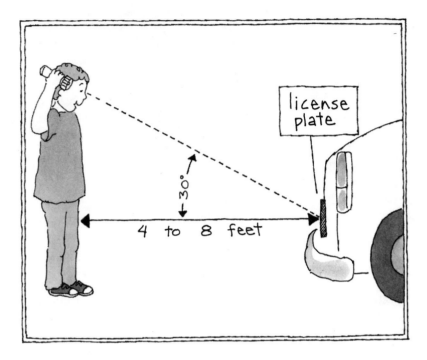

license plate

30°

4 to 8 feet

## Insider Information

The secret symbols are hidden in the reflective sheeting that covers the plate. The sheeting has a layer of tiny glass beads embedded in clear plastic. Behind the beads is a mirrorlike coating. When viewed from most angles, this coating reflects back just about all the light that strikes it.

However, the beads in the pattern of the secret image are treated so that they don't reflect any light when viewed from an angle of thirty degrees. The nonreflecting beads make up the dark areas of the secret pattern.

The reflective sheeting is provided to the states by

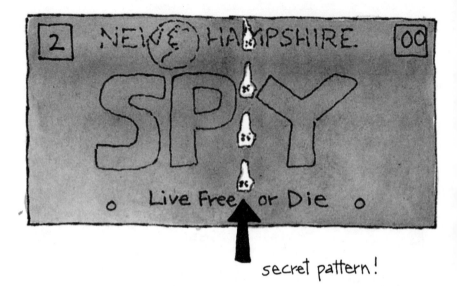

secret pattern!

the 3M Corporation, the only company that makes it. The manufacturing process is so sophisticated that it is unlikely that crooks will be able to duplicate it. Holograms on credit cards serve the same purpose as the secret images on license plates.

# THE GLUE CLUE

## Reveal hidden fingerprints with Krazy Glue.

*Where:* Yard
*Special Conditions:* Nice weather

## Doing the Deed

> **CAUTION!** Do this activity outdoors with an adult assistant. The fumes from Krazy Glue are toxic. The package warning reads "Avoid prolonged breathing of vapors. Use with adequate ventilation."
>
> Also, be very careful when handling Krazy Glue. If you accidentally get some on your skin, you can remove it with nail polish remover.

This is state-of-the-art forensic science. Detectives use Krazy Glue to uncover hidden fingerprints. So can you. Fingerprints will show up best on a dark-colored object.

You will need:

a box with a lid
a small square of aluminum foil or
   the lid of a jar
Krazy Glue
an object with fingerprints on it
clear tape
dark paper

cookie jar lid to be investigated

Find a box that comes with a lid. A fish tank with a glass cover is ideal because you can see the fingerprints developing. However, a cardboard box will also work. Make a shallow dish out of a piece of aluminum foil or use a disposable jar cover. Put the suspicious object inside the box at one end. Pour a puddle of Krazy Glue in the foil or jar cover and place it inside at the other end of the box. Cover the box so that the fumes don't escape. Let it sit in a warm place for several hours. Any fingerprints will show up as white images against the dark background.

## Insider Information

The active ingredient in Krazy Glue is cyanoacrylate. Fumes from this compound contain a chemical that bonds with the oil in fingerprints to produce a white material. The white fingerprint can be transferred to a piece of paper. Use a strip of clear cellophane tape to lift it and stick it onto a piece of dark-colored paper.

TRANSFER THE PRINT TO BLACK PAPER

Each person in the world—even identical twins—has his or her own set of fingerprint patterns. Fingerprints are so unique, they can be used to identify individuals. The FBI divides fingerprints into three basic patterns: loops, whorls, and arches.

LOOP          WHORL          ARCH

To make sure that the glue clue isn't you, fingerprint yourself. To get a clear print, press a finger on an ink pad (the kind you use with rubber stamps). Then gently roll your inked finger once on a white piece of paper. Don't roll your finger back and forth, or you'll smudge the fingerprint. If you don't have an ink pad, you can also rub a pencil on a piece of paper to make a large patch of graphite, then rub your finger on the graphite. Lift off the fingerprint with some clear cellophane tape and stick it on a piece of white paper. Inspect your fingerprint with a magnifying glass to see if you're a loop, whorl, or arch. Compare the pattern of your print to the print you lifted from the suspicious object. If the prints don't match, fingerprint other likely suspects.

# STINK BOMB

**Turn an ordinary balloon into a secret source of stink.**

*Where:* A yard or someone else's house
*Special Conditions:* None

## Doing the Deed

Don't do this at home, because it's more fun if you do it where there's a crowd. Stink bombs can be made in the stench of your choice, or they can be an unexpected, pleasant smell.

You will need:

>        several balloons
>        cotton swabs
>        clove of garlic
>        vanilla extract or perfume

Our favorite offensive odor is garlic. Crush a clove of garlic and roll a cotton swab in the juice. Rub the swab on the inside of a balloon. Don't rub it too close to the opening of the balloon, though. Remember, you have to blow up the balloon.

After you inflate the secret stinker, tie it off and put a string on it. Place it where lots of people walk by. Soon you will see them wrinkle their noses and try to

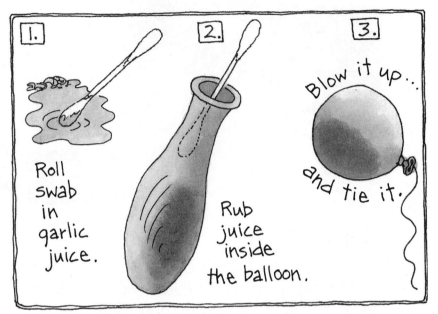

1. Roll swab in garlic juice.

2. Rub juice inside the balloon.

3. Blow it up... and tie it.

figure out where the smell is coming from.

To make an equally mysterious, but this time pleasant, smell, rub some vanilla extract or perfume inside a balloon.

Given a choice, we prefer garlic.

## Insider Information

Believe it or not, a balloon is full of tiny holes called pores. The pores are smaller than air molecules but larger than those mighty little garlic or perfume molecules. The garlic molecules seep through the balloon in a process called *osmosis*—the movement of molecules through a membrane. Then they spread rapidly through the air in another process called *diffusion*. Heat speeds up both processes—put the balloon near a lightbulb to accelerate the effect.

# RECIPE FOR A MUMMY

**Immortalize a piece of potato for future viewing (not eating).**

*Where:* Yard
*Special Conditions:* Nice weather

## Doing the Deed

Traditionally, a mummy is a dead body, human or animal, that has been preserved. Breaking with tradition, you can make a *vegetable* mummy. This recipe for creating a potato mummy is almost exactly like the one used by the ancient Egyptians to mummify bodies. It will keep bacteria from rotting the vegetable remains.

TATER TUT

You will need:

> 1/2 cup baking soda
> 1/2 cup washing soda (found in
>     the detergent section of the
>     supermarket)
> 1/4 cup salt
> a plastic cup
> a spoon
> a slice of potato
> plastic wrap

Mix the baking soda, washing soda, and salt together in the plastic cup, using the spoon. Then lay the slice of potato to rest in the plastic cup "tomb." Cover the cup securely with the plastic wrap. Bury the future mummy in the ground.

Mix sodas and salt.

plastic wrap

potato slice

sodas and salt

To make this more scientific, cut two more slices of potato. Bury one beside your embalmed specimen. Place the other on the surface of the ground.

Wait ten days. Then examine all your potato slices for signs of rot and decay.

## Insider Information

Mummification is an amazing method of preservation that has been used by humans for four or five thousand years. It also occurs naturally, through freezing, drying, or preservation in peat bogs or oil seeps. Some natural mummies are more than twenty-five thousand years old. The Egyptians practiced artificial mummification. They removed the body fluids with a kind of washing soda called *natron*. Then they put herbs and spices into the body before it was wrapped in linen. The process took seventy days.

Water is contained in every cell of every living thing, and removing it without damaging the body is not easy. But it can be drawn out chemically with salts. Washing soda, baking soda, and table salt are all part of the group of chemicals known as salts. Why would you want to remove water from the body? Bacteria that cause decay cannot grow where there is no water.

So Tater Tut is now officially a mummy.

*Caution!* Raccoons are known to be hazardous to the survival of potato mummies. Our neighborhood raccoons are notorious grave robbers.

# A CLEAN GETAWAY

**Walk on top of a liquid without getting your feet wet.**

*Where:* Yard, patio, or deck
*Special Conditions:* Nice weather

## Doing the Deed

Cornstarch and water—treat this mixture gently and it's a liquid; beat on it and it's a solid. Use this knowledge to do a phenomenal feat with your feet. But do this outside because it can be messy.

You will need:

> 1 box cornstarch
> 2 or more large baking pans (about
>     15" x 10")—1 for each step you take
> newspapers
> measuring cup
> water

Spread newspapers on the ground, because you might not get this right the first time. You'll have to clean up the mess when you're finished. Pour about two cups of water into one of the baking pans. Sprinkle in a package of cornstarch a little at a time, mixing with your hands. This mixture has been called *ooblick* or *gobbledygook*. Ooblick is the proper consistency when it is about as thick as mayonnaise. It should be about one inch deep. Repeat the mixing process in each pan you are using.

Set the pans about one footstep apart on the newspapers. Make sure your shoes are clean. Wipe the soles with wet rags or paper towels if necessary. Prepare mentally. You must be bold. Success comes only to those who stomp hard and fast. With forceful energy step into the pan and move quickly to the next. Don't stop until you're finished. Now check your shoes. If you walked on top of the ooblick, your shoes will be perfectly clean and dry. Pussyfooters are exposed by the ooblick on their soles.

# Insider Information

By now, you've probably noticed that the combination of cornstarch and water is not an ordinary mixture. The cornstarch doesn't dissolve in water. Why not? Each grain of cornstarch contains two kinds of structures—one is shaped like a crystal and the other is noncrystalline. The noncrystalline structures absorb more water than the crystalline. When the mixture is handled—in this case when you stomp on it—the crystalline structures break down and become noncrystalline. More water is then absorbed and the ooblick becomes solid. When the pressure is off, the crystals re-form, releasing the water, and the ooblick oozes once again.

Treading softly doesn't put enough pressure on the cornstarch to break the crystals. You'll get wet feet, as you would with a normal liquid. Stomping makes ooblick solid. If you stomp hard enough, you may actually crack it.

Ooblick is fun to play with. Roll it between your hands, and it becomes a ball. But don't try to throw an ooblick ball. As soon as you stop rolling it, ooblick drips through your fingers.

CAUTION! Do not dispose of your ooblick down any drain. Do not empty it into the toilet or the sink. It can form a solid plug and clog the pipes. Seal it in a plastic bag and throw it in the garbage.

# SUN RISER

**Use the sun to launch a hot-air balloon.**

*Where:* Yard
*Special Conditions:* Windless, sunny day

## Doing the Deed

Flying garbage bags? That's a funny thought. But it's possible. A garbage bag can become a hot-air balloon. You, as ground crew, will need to wait for a sunny day with no wind. Shake open a large, dark, plastic garbage bag in a cool, shady place. Hold it open and pull it through the air until it is almost fully inflated. Close it with a string or a twist tie. Attach a short leash of string.

Tie the bag down in a sunny place and wait. The bag will struggle to get off the ground as the sun's rays heat it. It will expand and become lighter than the air surrounding it. You'll eventually get a rise out of your sun-warmed garbage bag.

## Insider Information

Hot-air balloons rise because the hot air weighs less than an equal volume of cool air. The key to heating your balloon is the black surface of the garbage bag.

Dark colors absorb heat rays from the sun. The air inside the balloon gets warmer and expands. Because the same amount of material is now taking up more space, the air inside the garbage bag is less dense than the outside air. So the garbage bag is now light enough to float.

Consider having a collection of garbage bag balloons for your next birthday party.

# SUNBURNED BALLOONS

**The ultimate in overkill! Use thermonuclear energy to burst a balloon.**

*Where:* Yard
*Special Conditions:* Sunny day

## Doing the Deed

An innocent balloon is your target. A magnifying glass or Fresnel lens is your ray gun. And the blazing sun is your firepower in this blast of science fun.

You will need:

> balloon
> tape
> magnifying glass or Fresnel lens

Tape an inflated balloon down in a sunny spot. Position your lens between the balloon and the sun. Focus the rays of the sun into a bright spot on the balloon.

CAUTION! Do this with an adult assistant. The bright spot is concentrated heat and light energy! Do not stare directly at it, and do not focus it on any part of your body or on anything flammable. The temperature in this focused spot of sunlight can reach thousands of degrees.

30

This incredible heat will burn through the rubber in a split second, popping the balloon. A sunburned balloon pops so quickly you might want to challenge your friends to a balloon-bursting race.

## Insider Information

The sun's energy comes from an unbelievably enormous thermonuclear explosion that has been going on for billions of years. The distance of 93 million miles between the earth and the sun protects us from its destructive forces. Lenses bend light, and magnifying lenses are designed to bend light rays so that they come together at a single point. This concentrates the energy into a hot spot that can burn through rubber. Magnifying lenses can also be used to start fires. For this reason, they were once called burning glasses.

The shape of the magnifying lens determines how it will focus light. A simple glass magnifier is thicker in the center than it is at the edges. A Fresnel lens does the same thing as a magnifying lens. But instead of being a curved surface, a Fresnel lens is flat, with a series of concentric circles or ridges cut into it. Each ridge has a tiny bit of curvature. If you could put all the ridges next to one another and eliminate the grooves, you would have a lens with the same shape as a glass magnifier, but it would be much fatter.

Fresnel lenses are found in bar code scanners at supermarket checkout counters, in overhead projectors, and on the fronts of traffic lights.

# WITCH WAY TO THE WATER?

## Discover if you have dowsing talent.

## Doing the Deed

Dowsing is an ancient way of finding hidden water. Water witches, as they are sometimes called, search for underground sources of water with a variety of objects. The most common are a pendulum on a string, a forked stick, and two swiveling L-shaped rods. There are almost as many ways of dowsing as there are dowsers. A tried-and-true method is to hold a Y-shaped stick by the short ends with the long part parallel to the ground, and then walk over the ground until the stick points downward. Dowsers claim that the stick moves by itself when it is over water. Dowsers also say that not everyone is equal when it comes to dowsing ability.

pendulum     stick     bottles + coat-hanger wire

See if you have a gift for water witching. Hold a dowsing rod and walk toward water. Even a puddle will do if you're talented. If you're successful at puddle dowsing, move on and see if you can find the pipes buried in your yard.

## Insider Information

Some people think that dowsing is a hoax. But there is some evidence that it might work. In Southeast Asia, a dowser pointed out 691 well sites of which 664 yielded water—that's 96 percent accuracy. A German water witch has been 100 percent successful since 1980. In California, well drillers who used dowsers were reported to be twice as successful as those who didn't.

Dowsing has been defined as searching for anything in a way that does not use the five senses. Just how or if it works, no one knows. But water is not the only hidden treasure that dowsers claim to have found. Many of them say they have located valuable minerals, buried pipelines, lost keys, and even hidden tumors.

# 2

## School Activities:
### In a Class by Themselves

# BE A STILLIE PRODUCER

**Make the opposite of a movie.**

*Where:* Classroom
*Special Conditions:* None

## Doing the Deed

A moving picture is an illusion. It is nothing more than a rapid sequence of still pictures. When the pictures are flashed at a rate of twenty-four images per second, you can't see the individual pictures. Instead, you see the sequence as continuous motion.

It is possible to make the opposite of a movie—a series of movements that produce a still picture. What do you call the opposite of a movie? We came up with "stillie," but maybe you can do better.

You will need:

> slide projector or overhead projector
> slide with an image on it
> sheet of paper
> yardstick
> overhead transparency film
> stiff piece of white paper or a foam
> > board

You will need to project an image. A slide projector or an overhead projector will do. You don't, however, need a screen. Position the projector so that the light beam goes out a window or through an open doorway. You want the light to go off into the distance and not fall on a nearby surface.

Put a slide in the projector. Hold a piece of paper in the beam of light about five feet from the projector. Have a friend focus the image on the paper. Remove the paper. You can't see any picture now. But it's there. Prove it by rapidly waving a yardstick up and down at the same spot you held the piece of paper.

The image appears, hanging in thin air.

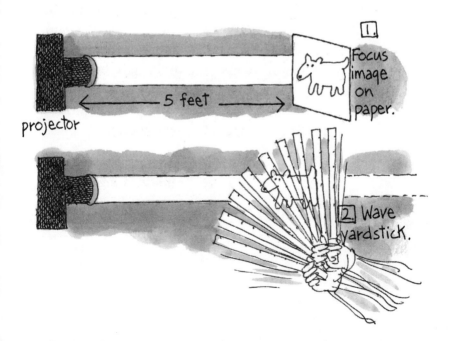

projector

← — 5 feet — →

1. Focus image on paper.

2. Wave yardstick.

# Insider Information

If you hold the yardstick in the light beam, you will see a very thin band of the image on the stick. By rapidly moving the yardstick up and down, you produce a series of bands, each showing a different part of the picture. After an image disappears, your eye retains it for about 1/30 of a second. If the yardstick makes a sweep from top to bottom in 1/30 of a second, there are enough bands to fuse into a single image. By waving the stick up and down at least sixteen times a second, the fused image remains visible.

When you wave the yardstick up and down, you are creating a flat surface. What if you move it with a circular motion? You will get a distorted image. The picture will curve as if it were being projected onto a globe.

You can also make an imaginary cylinder from a flat circle. Draw a circle on overhead transparency film. Set up the experiment the same way as you did for the yardstick activity. This time, instead of a yardstick, use a piece of stiff white paper or foam board. Hold the paper or foam board in the light beam with the flat side toward the projector. Move it rapidly toward and away from the projector. Your motion makes the flat circle appear to be a cylinder.

← Move board back and forth. →

# LOONY TUNES

## A computer monitor makes a rigid tuning fork wiggle weirdly.

*Where:* Computer lab
*Special Conditions:* None

## Doing the Deed

School is a good place to create this "metal bending" illusion because you are likely to find both a tuning fork and a computer monitor there. Borrow the tuning fork from the music room or from the science teacher. Take it to a computer monitor. Turn on the monitor and the computer. Create a blank screen on the monitor by opening a new file.

Hold the tuning fork by its handle. Gently strike it against a desk to make it vibrate. Look at it as the tone sounds. Now move it in front of the monitor. Hold the tuning fork vertically. The tines appear to be distorted with a wavelike motion. Hold it horizontally, and you get a different effect—the tines appear to be vibrating slowly.

## Insider Information

A computer monitor screen (or a television) looks as though it is illuminated by a steady light, but it's not.

A tiny beam of light scans back and forth across the screen from top to bottom sixty times a second. Every point on the screen is illuminated sixty times each second. The rest of the time it is dark. But your eyes see this as continuous light because they aren't sensitive enough to see such rapid flickering.

A rapidly flickering light is called a *strobe.* A strobe appears to slow down moving objects. When something moves in front of a strobe, the on-off flashes capture the object in multiple positions, and it appears to be several objects instead of a single moving one.

A monitor is a complicated kind of strobe. Because of the scanning nature of the monitor's light, an additional illusion is created. This special effect is only visible when the tuning fork is held vertically and is vibrating faster than sixty times a second. It is especially visible when the vibrating frequency (measured in hertz) of the tuning fork is close to some whole-number multiple of sixty. Then the solid metal of the tines appears to bend in a wave formation—and the waves appear to travel down the tines as the scanner moves from top to bottom. The multiple images of the vibrating tines are in different positions as the scanner moves down the screen. This causes the wave effect.

You can see a similar effect with a rubber band. Cut one open to make a rubber string. Have a friend stretch it tightly and hold it vertically in front of a monitor. Pluck the string and watch what happens.

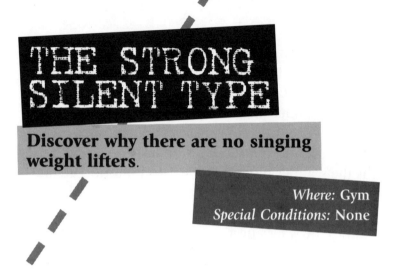

# THE STRONG SILENT TYPE

**Discover why there are no singing weight lifters.**

*Where:* Gym
*Special Conditions:* None

## Doing the Deed

Have your gym teacher select an activity that requires upper body strength, such as push-ups, chin-ups, or weight lifting. Choose a song everyone knows, and see if anyone is able to sing it while doing the chosen workout.

Instead of music, you'll get grunts.

## Insider Information

When you want to lift a heavy weight, you need to tense the muscles in your chest and abdomen. You do this by holding your breath. It increases the pressure in your chest cavity, and your ribs become a more stable platform for the muscles to pull against. This increases their lifting power. This strength-enhancing technique is called the *Valsalva maneuver.*

During the Valsalva maneuver, a little flap called the *epiglottis* closes your windpipe. And the windpipe is directly related to your ability to sing, because sounds are produced when air moves past your vocal cords, which are located below the epiglottis. Since the epiglottis is closed when you are straining, no air can move. So you can't sing.

The song of strain is a grunt—a sound the dictionary says is "short, deep and typical of pigs."

# FALLING FOR BOYS

**Most boys will fall for this trick, but girls usually won't.**

*Where:* Classroom, gym
*Special Conditions:* None

## Doing the Deed

This activity separates the boys from the girls. Do it with a large group, and see what happens.

Each participant should kneel on the floor and bend forward with the elbows against the knees and with the hands together in a praying position. Have an assistant stand a matchbox on end and place it in front of the fingertips. Once the matchbox is in place, everyone should go back to the original kneeling position and clasp hands behind the back.

Now for the test. Each participant must lean forward and try to knock over the matchbox using only the nose.

Some participants will be able to knock over the matchbox. Some will fall on their faces! In general, the boys will do most of the falling.

## Insider Information

This is a balancing act. In order to keep from falling on your face, you have to keep your center of gravity from getting too far in front of your knees. In boys, the center of gravity is usually higher up than it is in girls. For the most part, males have more mass in their upper bodies than in their lower bodies, and this makes them somewhat top-heavy. Girls usually have more of their weight in their hips. The heavier hips are a counterweight and allow females to lean out farther.

There will probably be exceptions in your test group. See if you can figure out why.

# SMART BUBBLES

*Where:* Classroom, science lab
*Special Conditions:* None

## Doing the Deed

Begin your quest for smart bubbles by searching for a Van de Graaff generator. This machine, used to demonstrate electrostatic experiments, is often found in high-school physics classrooms. If your school doesn't have one, perhaps your teacher can arrange to borrow one.

> CAUTION! Van de Graaff generators can give you a shock. Do this experiment with the help of an adult.

When you've found a Van de Graaff generator, have your adult assistant turn it on. Blow a stream of soap bubbles toward the generator. The bubbles will be attracted to the negatively charged sphere until the lead bubble strikes it and pops. At this point, the others will turn tail and run away, as if they had gotten the message, "Electricity can be hazardous to your health."

# Insider Information

If you think soap bubbles are smart, you may be a bubblehead. Obviously there is some other explanation for this unexpected bubble behavior. It's static electricity.

Here's what's happening. The Van de Graaff generator produces a strong electric field of force around itself by collecting electrons on its metal sphere. Since all electrons are negatively charged particles, the electrostatic field of force is also negatively charged. When soap bubbles enter the field, their electrons move away from the generator because like charges repel each other. Without electrons, the side of each soap bubble facing the generator becomes positively charged. Now the bubbles are attracted to the generator because opposite charges attract. When the first bubble strikes the generator, it instantly picks up electrons and becomes negatively charged for the rest of its extremely short life. But its influence extends after its bubble phase. When the lead bubble pops, droplets of the negatively charged soapy water spray onto the approaching bubbles. They in turn pick up the negative charge and are then repelled by the electric field.

# MUSCLE TONES

**Listen to the rumble, crackle, and pop of muscles.**

*Where:* Auditorium, gym
*Special Conditions:* None

## Doing the Deed

People have known about strange rumblings from inside the body for hundreds of years—sounds that are different from the loud gurgles of the digestive tract. They heard them by putting their thumbs in their ears and clenching their fists. Try it. You, too, will hear faint rumbles and crunches. At first, no one knew these were the sounds of muscles working.

We have learned a lot about these sounds with the aid of modern technology. Scientists use an electronic stethoscope to detect muscle tones, but you can use the microphone and speakers of a public address system.

Muscle sounds have been described as crackles, a series of clicks, and low rumbles. To hear them for yourself, have someone hold a two- to five-pound weight with an outstretched arm. (A weight makes the muscles work harder and maximizes their sounds.) Place a microphone against your assistant's biceps. You may have to move the microphone

around to find the noisiest spot. Also, if your speakers are adjustable, set them to amplify the bass tones.

## Insider Information

There are two reasons why it's hard to hear muscle tones without some electronic help. First, they aren't very loud. Second, their deep pitch is at the lower limit of human hearing. Although an ordinary stethoscope or a mike and speakers amplify sound, we still miss many low frequencies. An electronic stethoscope is used because it is able to change low-frequency muscle sounds into visible lines on a screen.

Some animals hear low-frequency sounds a lot better than humans do. Sharks, for example. Recent studies have shown they are attracted to prey by the noise of their muscles, not their thrashing movements. That may be why they can locate even quietly swimming prey.

Sound travels much better in water than it does in air, so under water may be the best place to listen to your muscles. Submerge your head and open and close a hand near your ear. Now you can hear the sound of one hand clapping.

# TROUBLED WATERS

**See the tension dissolve between two liquids.**

*Where:* Classroom
*Special Conditions:* None

## Doing the Deed

Watch as two liquids battle for supremacy.

You will need:

- overhead projector
- Pyrex glass dish
- water
- food coloring
- teaspoon
- rubbing alcohol

The war zone is a Pyrex glass dish placed on an overhead projector. To prepare for battle, pour a thin layer of water into the dish. Stain it with a few drops of your favorite food coloring. Turn on the projector and focus the image on a wall or screen. Now, drop about a half teaspoon of rubbing alcohol into the center of the colored water.

The water retreats from the alcohol, and the alcohol follows, leaving a clear, dry spot in the center of the dish. Watch the struggle between the two liquids

Add ½ teaspoon of rubbing alcohol to the colored water.

food coloring

← water

at the borderline where they meet. Eventually the liquids merge, and the troubled waters are peaceful again.

## Insider Information

The tension of the liquids is real. It is called *surface tension*. The molecules on a liquid's surface cling together and act like a skin. Both the water and the rubbing alcohol have surface tension, but water's is stronger. When you drop in the rubbing alcohol, you're creating a surface of alcohol in the middle of the water. The water pulls away because, with its stronger surface tension, it is more attracted to itself than to the alcohol. With its weaker surface tension, the alcohol is more attracted to the water than to itself. So the alcohol follows the water, leaving a dry spot. But this is only the beginning.

How is the conflict of warring liquids resolved? Solution is the solution. Alcohol dissolves in water. The activity at the borderline is created as the alcohol and water mix. Eventually, the alcohol spreads evenly throughout the water. Only then does the new alcohol-water solution move over the dry spot and re-form an unbroken surface.

# STRESS TEST

## Doing the Deed

Lots of materials can get stressed out, and you know what happens then. Failure! Overstressed things tend to break. You can easily detect stress points in transparent plastic with polarized sunglasses.

Put on a pair of polarized sunglasses. Hold the other pair in front of you and slowly rotate it clockwise. You will notice that there is a position where all the light is blocked and the lenses of the pair you are holding look black. Keep holding the sunglasses in this position.

Put a piece of transparent plastic in front of one of the lenses. (Good sources of plastic to stress test are jewel boxes for CDs, cassette cases, clear plastic forks, or even torn plastic bags.) Look at areas that are bent, at edges, and at stamped designs. If you don't see any stress, apply some by bending, breaking, or tearing the plastic. In sunlight stressed areas will appear in a rainbow of colors with the most stressed areas appearing as black lines. Because the colors can inter-

fere with the detection of the stresses, it is better to use a light source that is a single color, such as the sodium- or mercury-vapor bulbs in streetlamps. Only the black lines will show up under these lights.

## Insider Information

Finding hidden stresses may not seem like an earth-shaking discovery to you, but architects in California think it is. They worry about metal fatigue, a kind of weakness, in the structures they design for earth-quake zones. Before a design is finalized, a clear plastic model is subjected to forces similar to an earth-quake and then examined using polarized lenses. The weak points in the model predict problems that could occur in a real building.

Materials that are not transparent can also be examined for stress—but not with polarized lenses. Airplanes and bridges, which can develop metal fatigue, are regularly inspected with X rays.

# 3

# Park Amusements and Amusement Parks

# "G" WHIZ

## Measure the g-forces on a roller coaster.

*Where:* Amusement park
*Special Conditions:* None

## Doing the Deed

Astronauts must withstand three times the force of gravity, or 3 g's, to get into orbit. You can experience more than that without leaving the planet. There's no better place to feel g-forces than on a roller coaster. Some of them are even designed to give you a 4-g thrill.

You always experience at least 1 g. That's the force of gravity pulling on you when you're standing still. When you change your speed over a short period of time, or accelerate, you feel a change in the g-force on your body. As you accelerate forward in the roller coaster, your seat presses against your back, but you feel as if you are being pushed back into your seat. As you accelerate upward, you feel heavier as your seat cushion presses up against your body. You can measure the amount of g-force with a home-made accelerometer.

You will need:

        G-Meter Scale (see instructions
           below)
        paper
        scissors
        tape
        protractor
        string
        heavy washer

Copy the diagram of the G-Meter Scale on page 59 onto a piece of plain paper, cut it out, and tape it to the back of the protractor. Tie one end of the string in the center of the straight edge of the protractor. Tie the washer to the other end of the string so that it hangs about two inches below the curved edge of the protractor. Take the G-Meter Scale along on your next trip to an amusement park.

To use your accelerometer, hold it at a right angle to your body with the straight edge at the top and parallel to the ground. The washer will be hanging down with the string positioned at zero. As you accelerate in the roller coaster, the string will move backward. Read the amount of g-force on your G-Meter Scale.

# Insider Information

The human body was designed to operate at 1 g. It is still fairly comfortable at 2 g's. At 6 g's most people get nosebleeds. At 9 g's they lose consciousness, because chest muscles aren't strong enough for breathing, and the heart isn't strong enough to push the blood around. However, U.S. Air Force experiments have shown that the human body can take 30 g's for a few seconds and survive without permanent injury.

The greatest acceleration on a regular roller coaster is at the bottom of a straight drop. If there's a loop, the g-forces are greatest just as you enter the loop. Notice that roller coasters don't have circular loops. If they did, the coaster would have to have a g-force of at least 6.5 to stay on the track at the top of the loop when it's upside-down. A teardrop-shaped loop reduces the needed g-force to 4 g's or less and keeps the riders safe.

Amusement parks aren't the only place where g-forces are in action. Take your accelerometer with you on an airplane. During takeoff, the airplane accelerates from 0 to about 150 miles an hour before it leaves the ground.

Check out the school bus as it leaves the launch pad. You'll be lucky to see half a g.

# G-METER SCALE

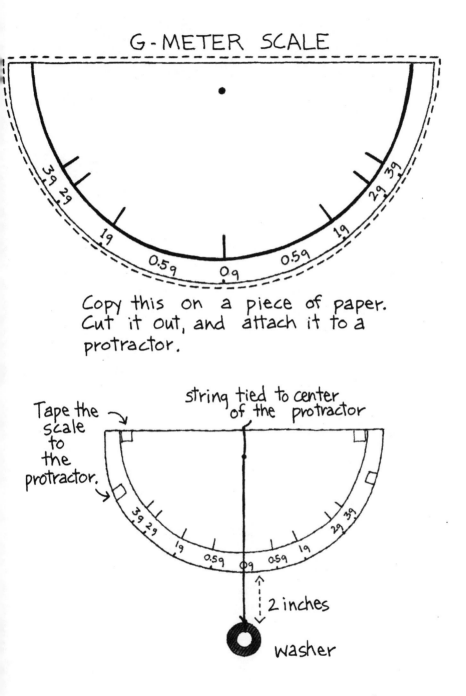

3g 2g 1g 0.5g 0g 0.5g 1g 2g 3g

Copy this on a piece of paper.
Cut it out, and attach it to a
protractor.

string tied to center of the protractor

Tape the
scale
to
the
protractor.

3g 2g 1g 0.5g 0g 0.5g 1g 2g 3g

2 inches

washer

# QUICK COMEDOWN

## Use a tiny dent to destroy the strength of a soda can.

*Where:* Playground, paved driveway
*Special Conditions:* None

## Doing the Deed

The thin wall of an empty aluminum soda can is strong enough to support your weight—if you weigh less than 250 pounds. However, it's strong enough only if your weight is evenly distributed on top of the can. You'll need a perfect can, too. One with no dents in it.

This balancing act is a bit tricky. The easiest way to get up on the can is with the help of a couple of friends. Place one foot on top of the can. Hang on to your friends (always a good idea), and lift your other foot off the ground, gently transferring all your weight onto the can.

When you are balanced, have one of your friends tap the side of the can with the eraser end of a pencil. It doesn't take much of an effort. The can will instantly collapse. Talk about a quick comedown!

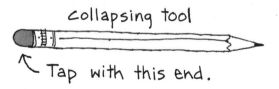

collapsing tool

↖ Tap with this end.

> **CAUTION!** Do this outside on a hard, level surface. Don't do this at home, because you might slip off the can and send it—or yourself—rocketing into furniture or other breakable objects, including humans.

## Insider Information

An aluminum can, with walls no thicker than two pieces of paper, can support eight thousand times its own weight. It is essential, however, that the center of the load be directly over the center of the can. Your weight may be heavy enough to cause the sides of the can to bulge. But it won't collapse as long as your weight is evenly distributed.

A dent in the can creates a weak spot. Then the weight from above pushes the dent farther out of line, and the can collapses into a nice flat pancake, ready for recycling.

# SPIN DOCTOR

**Speed up a merry-go-round by throwing your weight around.**

*Where:* Playground
*Special Conditions:* Nice weather

## Doing the Deed

Get a high-performance ride out of a playground merry-go-round—the kind you push. Beefing up the ride will take a few friends, one for each triangular section of the merry-go-round. Everybody needs to push, and then jump on when the ride is moving as fast as all of you can get it to go. The riders should keep to the outside. Notice the speed of the merry-go-round. Then, at the count of three, have everyone shift to the center. If you all move at the same time, the merry-go-round will spin faster.

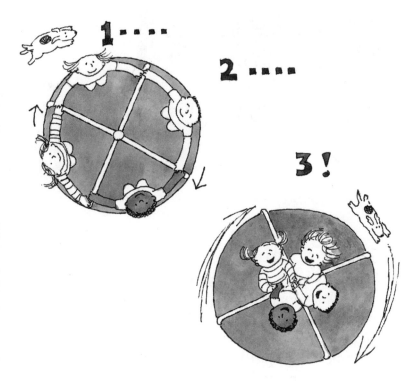

# Insider Information

A merry-go-round spins around a central post called the *axis of rotation*. The rate at which it spins is determined by how weight is distributed around the axis of rotation. The closer the weight is to the center, the faster the merry-go-round goes.

Spinning ice-skaters take advantage of this physics principle. By pulling their arms close to their bodies, they speed up and turn into whirling blurs. Gymnasts know the secret of rapid spinning, too. The tighter they tuck, the faster they can rotate and the more turns they can get into a flip.

# SWING TIME

**Discover which takes longer: swinging in a big arc or swinging in a little one.**

*Where:* Playground
*Special Conditions:* Nice weather

## Doing the Deed

Take a guess. In a swinging contest who do you think would take longer to make two complete swings: a pumped-up high swinger or a gently swaying rider? You'll probably guess wrong. This is a no-win contest.

Some things just have to be seen to be believed, and this is one of them. You can use two swings side by side or a single swing to conduct the experiment. If you use two swings, it is important that their ropes or chains be the same length. It is not necessary that

the swingers be the same weight. Use a watch that times seconds or count off the seconds by saying: One chimpanzee, two chimpanzee, etc.

Get both swings going—one high and fast, the other slow and low. Then have the riders quit pumping and let the swings move naturally. Time how long it takes for each rider to return to the place you started measuring from. There are no winners here. But there are no losers either. Big arc swings and little arc swings take exactly the same amount of time.

## Insider Information

To understand what is going on, you have to get physical. To a physicist, a swing is simply a pendulum. The time it takes for the pendulum to make one complete to-and-fro swing is called its *period*. The period of a pendulum is affected only by the pendulum's length. The distance it moves or the weight it moves has absolutely no effect.

Before mechanical clocks were invented, the Italian physicist Galileo discovered this law of pendulum motion. He noticed a swinging lamp in church and timed its period by using his pulse. He found that the period of the lamp remained the same even as it slowly decreased the distance it swung. This seemingly useless bit of trivia was later used by clockmakers. Pendulums became the basis for measuring time. It's a good thing Galileo didn't get too excited by his discovery. If his heart had begun to beat faster and his pulse had speeded up, the march of science might never have been the same.

# AIMLESS FUN

**Experience the illusion of throwing a curveball while remaining a straight shooter.**

*Where:* Playground
*Special Conditions:* Nice weather

## Doing the Deed

A simple game of catch becomes a whole new ball game when you're going around in circles. Try as you will, throwing a ball that can be caught by a catcher isn't easy if you are on a merry-go-round.

Play catch with a friend when you are both on a moving merry-go-round. Carefully aim a tennis or other soft ball, and throw. The ball will appear to curve away from your friend.

Another variation of aimless fun is to throw to a catcher standing a distance away from the merry-go-round. Again, a miss.

## Insider Information

When you're playing catch on a merry-go-round, the path of the ball is determined by more than one factor. Take the first pitch—throwing to someone else on the merry-go-round. Your position relative to the catcher doesn't change. But you are both moving. When you release the ball, it travels away from you in a straight line. However, your targeted catcher is circling. In the time it takes the ball to reach the spot you aimed at, the catcher has moved. So the ball misses the target and appears to be traveling in a curved path. In reality, though, it's the background that's moving in relation to you.

In the second pitch—thrown from a rotating merry-go-round to a stationary catcher—the ball has two forces operating on it that affect its path. One is the force you deliver with your mighty muscles. The other is delivered by the spinning merry-go-round. The two forces acting together throw off your throw.

To hit the target if you're going clockwise, aim to the right of the friend who is moving with you on the merry-go-round and to the left of the friend on the ground. With practice you can master merry-go-round catch.

# 4

# Going Public

# MIRACLE AT THE MALL

**Amaze a friend by extracting cola from an uncola drink.**

*Where:* Restaurant
*Special Conditions:* None

## Doing the Deed

Pull a fast one on a friend the next time you're in a fast-food restaurant. When your friend orders a drink, order a drink that's the same size but of a different color. In other words, if your friend orders a clear drink, you order a cola. Let your friend carry the food to the table while you carry the drinks. Of course you'll have to make a stop to get straws. Unwrap the straws and stick one down to the bottom of each beverage. Put a finger over the end of each straw and pull them both out of the cups. You will be holding a sample of soda in each straw. Switch the straws—put the one with the uncola sample into the cola and vice versa. Keep your fingers tightly on the tops of the straws until both straws touch the bottoms of the cups. The setup is now complete, and you can treat the cups as if there's nothing amiss.

Before your friend has a chance to drink the clear beverage, say, "Oh, look, they've gotten some cola in your drink. Let me see if I can get it out." Reach over and wiggle the straw, pretending to gather up the contaminating cola. Then put your finger on the top of the straw and lift it out. Hold the straw over an empty cup and release your finger. Miraculously, or so it seems, cola runs out of the straw.

If your friend starts drinking before you are able to work wonders, don't worry. Chances are he or she won't notice the change in flavors. In spite of what the advertisers say, one sweet fizzy soft drink tastes very much like another. Besides, you've got a back-up—your drink. Just say, "Oh, look, they've got some uncola in my cola...."

## Insider Information

This is no miracle. This is science in action. Air pressure keeps the soda in the straw. When the straw is sitting in the drink, the level of the soda in the straw is always exactly the same as the level of soda in the cup. The atmosphere presses equally on the surface of the liquid in the cup and in the straw. Cover the top of the straw and you cut off atmospheric pressure from above. The soda doesn't run out because the pressure on the bottom of the straw is now greater than gravity.

You might wonder why the cola in the straw doesn't mix with the uncola when you switch straws. It will...eventually. The reason it takes a long time to mix is that the only place where the two liquids are in contact with each other is at the end of the straw and this is a very small area. This gives you plenty of time to get your act together.

# STRAW-WRAPPER SNAKE

**Turn a soda straw wrapper into a writhing snake.**

## Doing the Deed

To create this lifelike creature, you need a soda straw in a paper wrapper. Hold the wrapped straw in a vertical position and grasp the top end between your thumb and index finger. Slide your fingers down the straw. The wrapper will split at the top end, and the paper will be scrunched together at the bottom. Pull off the wrapper, keeping it in its tightly compressed form. This is your new pet. Put it on a waterproof surface where it has room to grow.

Now dip the end of the straw into a beverage and cover the top of the straw with your finger to collect some liquid. You want to turn the straw into a dropper. You can control the amount of liquid that runs out of the bottom end of the straw by regulating the amount of air you let into the top end of it. Practice until you can release one drop at a time. Put a drop of liquid on the paper "snake." Water makes the snake move and grow. Add more drops. The snake will wriggle and squirm until it is completely wet.

# Insider Information

Paper is made up of thousands of tiny cellulose fibers. The fibers are bent when the paper is scrunched. Paper absorbs water easily. When this happens, the fibers swell and straighten out.

# GRASPING AT STRAWS

**Others may grasp at straws, but you can hold one with a completely open hand.**

*Where:* Restaurant
*Special Conditions:* None

## Doing the Deed

This is something you can do to amuse your dining companions in a restaurant that provides straws with paper wrappers. Tear off one end of the wrapper and push it up enough so that you can grasp the straw at the bottom. With your other hand, rapidly slide the paper wrapper up and down the straw. Five to ten times should be enough.

Remove the wrapper. Hold the hand that moved the wrapper in the position you would use to karate-chop a brick. Place the straw against your open palm, and let go with the other hand. Ta-da! The straw sticks without any grasping.

## Insider Information

You'll get a charge out of this explanation. In fact, by rubbing the straw and paper together you create an electric charge on both. Electricity produced by rubbing is called *static electricity.* Tiny negatively charged particles, known as *electrons,* rub off the paper wrapper onto the plastic straw. Since the straw now has an excess of electrons, it becomes negatively charged. The paper, having lost electrons, is now positively charged. Electric charges are either positive or negative. Opposite charges attract each other. Like charges repel each other.

Your hand has no charge. But when you bring the negatively charged straw near it, the electrons on your skin are pushed away from the surface, giving a slight positive charge to your hand. The straw is now attracted and sticks.

The straw will continue to stick as long as it remains charged. It will lose its charge as it leaks its extra electrons to your hand or to the air. Water molecules attract electrons. If both the weather and your hand are dry, you will be more successful than if your hand is moist and the humidity is high.

# THE TILTED TOILET

**How to detect the swaying motion of a skyscraper.**

*Where:* Skyscraper
*Special Conditions:* None

## Doing the Deed

Skyscrapers used to be called cloud scratchers. That's a good description for them, because the tops of these tall buildings move back and forth in the wind.

Even on the top floors of a skyscraper, which sway the most, you can't sense the motion. But you are moving—and you can prove it. Go to a rest room and look in the toilet. Believe it or not, a toilet can be a scientific instrument. The water gently tilts from one side of the bowl to the other as the building sways.

Keep this discovery to yourself if you don't want to explain why you've been toilet gazing.

## Insider Information

Things are not always what they seem to be. It appears that the water in the toilet is tilting from side to side. But it isn't moving at all. The toilet is moving around the water because the toilet is attached to the building and the building is swaying. Water, like all liquids, *always* has a surface that is parallel with the earth's surface. In other words, it is always level.

Modern skyscrapers are built to withstand forces. They are flexible enough to sway when the wind blows or an earthquake shakes them. The building's motion absorbs enough of the impact to prevent damage. In a really tall building the movement is not insignificant. The top of the World Trade Center in New York sways about twelve feet.

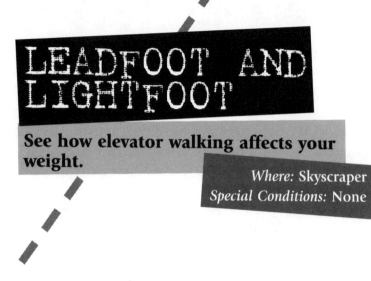

# LEADFOOT AND LIGHTFOOT

**See how elevator walking affects your weight.**

*Where:* Skyscraper
*Special Conditions:* None

## Doing the Deed

This is not a hands-on activity. We call it feet-on. Walk back and forth in a high-speed elevator as it accelerates upward. As you lift one foot, the other feels as if it is supporting more than its usual load. You'll also find that it's harder to jump when you're going up.

Going down, you'll no longer feel like a leadfooted walker but more like a lightfooted one. As in the upward journey, you can feel these changes only when the elevator is speeding up.

These feelings are not imaginary. The changes in weight can actually be measured. Bring along a bathroom scale. Stand on it and discover the ups and downs of elevator weight watching.

## Insider Information

When the elevator is speeding up as it is rising, it is pushing up with a force that is greater than your weight. You feel as if you are heavier, and so you push downward with a greater force than normal when you walk. The increased force is measured on the scale as an increase in your weight. The reverse happens when you are descending. The acceleration of the falling elevator is subtracted from the pull of gravity, making you feel and walk lighter.

YOU WEIGH MORE
GOING UP.

YOU WEIGH LESS
GOING DOWN.

# LIE OF THE LAND

## Confuse a compass in the library.

*Where:* Library
*Special Conditions:* None

## Doing the Deed

A library is a good place for finding things, but you don't need a compass there. In fact, a library security system can make a compass monumentally unreliable.

To discover what a mess you can make of your compass, take it to a library that has a magnetic security system. You can recognize this type of security system by the archway at the exit. Inside the library, look at your compass and make a mental note of where north is. Then take your compass to the front desk and ask the librarian to stroke it over the device the library uses to prepare the books for checkout. Look at your compass again. The north-seeking end of the needle now points south.

*Caution:* Don't use your lying compass to find your way home.

## Insider Information

You can find your way with a compass because the marked end of the needle points north. The reason it does this is that it is a magnet and so is the earth. The north-seeking pole of the compass needle is attracted to the earth's North Pole.

Some libraries put a strip of metal that has been encoded with a magnetic signal in each book. When the detector in the archway reads this signal, an alarm rings, which can be very embarrassing. Part of the checkout process includes stroking the book over a strong permanent magnet. The magnet scrambles the signal in the strip so that it doesn't trigger the alarm. When you return the book, another device demagnetizes the strip, which reactivates the encoded signal.

The checkout magnet is so powerful that it can scramble the smaller permanent magnet that is a compass needle. This is not a random scramble; the magnetic field does a 180-degree flip. Librarians treat the supermagnet with respect. It can erase magnetic tape, both audio and video, and damages mechanical watches.

Your compass is not broken. You can get it back on track with another pass over the supermagnet.

# 5

# Trains, Planes, and Automobiles

# RACING WITH THE MOON

**Race the moon in a car or train and you'll never win...or lose either.**

*Where:* Car, train, playground
*Conditions:* Clear night, full moon

## Doing the Deed

Look at the moon as you speed down the highway. You whiz by trees, houses, telephone poles, and people, but you can't get ahead of the moon. Increasing your speed won't help at all. Neither will slowing down. The moon appears to be traveling along with you. And you can't shake it.

## Insider Information

As you ride along, faraway objects stay in view longer than nearby objects. At a distance of 239,000 miles from the earth, the moon is definitely far away. So it is going to stay in your sight a very long time. You can't move far enough fast enough to change the angle of your view.

You can see this on a smaller scale on a playground. Position two friends one behind the other in the middle of the playground. The farther apart they are from each other, the better. Walk a path that is at right angles to an imaginary line connecting your friends, passing about ten feet in front of the closer one. Keep your head turned toward your friends as you walk. Your distant friend (a stand-in for the moon) will be in your line of sight much longer than your closer friend (a stand-in for the trees, houses, or telephone poles).

A lot of heavenly motion is actually going on while you are moon gazing. The earth is spinning on its axis, making the moon rise and set. The moon is revolving around the earth, displaying different amounts of its illuminated surface over the course of a month. But neither of these motions is fast enough to make a difference in what you see when you look out your car window.

# FALSE STARTS

**You feel as if you're on the move, but it's only in your mind.**

*Where:* Plane or train
*Special Conditions:* You are waiting at the station or on a plane

## Doing the Deed

Trains and planes have "windows of opportunity." Picture this. You are in a train waiting to leave the station. As you look out the window, you see a moving train on the next track. However, it doesn't appear to be moving. Instead, you feel certain that *your* train is pulling out of the station. Uh-uh! Time for a reality check. One look at the platform and you can see that you're *not* going anywhere yet. But look again at the other train, and you will feel the illusion of motion again.

## Insider Information

Your eyes are operating as they normally do as you view a moving object out the window of your stationary vehicle. They send information to the brain that lets you know something is in motion. But because the moving object fills your field of vision, your brain is not getting all the information it needs to determine which object is moving: you or the train you see out the window. Normally some stationary object would give you an additional clue, and your brain could make the correct decision. Without a clue, however, your brain is literally without a clue, too. It often sends false signals that the motion is your own. It is easy to trick the brain when it expects to experience some motion. After all, that's why you are on the train in the first place—to go somewhere.

We have also had this illusion when looking out the window of a parked airplane. Instead of a passing train, the moving object that tricked us was a luggage carrier.

You may also experience this illusion in IMAX theaters, which surround you with a moving picture. The scenes of roller coasters, dashing fire trucks, or small planes were deliberately chosen to create the false-start illusion and trick you into thinking that you are moving. Scientists call this little bit of brain confusion the *Duncker effect*, after the man who first described it.

# SUPERSONIC SONGS

## Doing the Deed

Would you believe you can hear music with a piece of paper?

Roll a piece of paper into a cone. Insert the small end of the cone into one of the little holes meant for the headset plug. Turn up the volume. There is no need to put your ear next to the cone. You will be able to hear the music from several aisles away.

## Insider Information

The music from a plane's sound system comes from a tiny speaker inside the armrest. You can hear the music if you put your ear on the armrest. However, you can't watch a movie from this position.

The speaker sets air in motion, making sound waves. Sound waves enter the small end of the cone and make the paper vibrate. As the waves move up the cone, more and more paper vibrates. This reinforces the sound, making it louder. See how far away you can hear the music.

88

An airline headset contains no electronic amplification system. An air-filled tube conducts the sound waves from the armrest to each ear. This is not the same system used in portable CD or tape player headsets. In these, the tiny speakers are actually in each earpiece. Although electronic earphones give a better sound, airlines use nonelectronic ones because they are cheaper to replace and can be sanitized between users.

You may find that this experiment works better on some planes than on others.

Plug cone or headset in here.

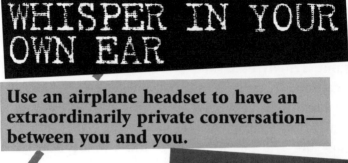

# WHISPER IN YOUR OWN EAR

## Use an airplane headset to have an extraordinarily private conversation—between you and you.

*Where:* Plane
*Special Conditions:* In flight

## Doing the Deed

Put on the headset, but don't plug it in. Instead, whisper into the plug. You will hear your secret message loud and clear.

You can also have a very private conversation with a friend. Both of you should put on headsets and then exchange plugs. Speak softly into your partner's plug. This is an especially good way to exchange

Testing... Testing... one.... two.... three.

secrets because the background noise of the plane's engines will keep others from overhearing.

## Insider Information

The earphones were designed to transmit sound from the speaker in the plane's armrest to your ears. But they're not exclusive. They will also transmit sounds from other sources, such as your voice.

The headphone tubes are hollow and filled with air. When sound waves enter the tubes, the air is set in motion and the sound is conducted to your ears. If you don't believe that this headset is low-tech, just blow into the plug while you're wearing it. Amazing! You can feel your own breath in your ears.

A stethoscope works in a similar fashion. It conducts sounds to a doctor's ears through two hollow tubes. We tried to use an airplane headset as a stethoscope but couldn't hear our hearts. Perhaps you will have better luck!

I read you loud and clear!

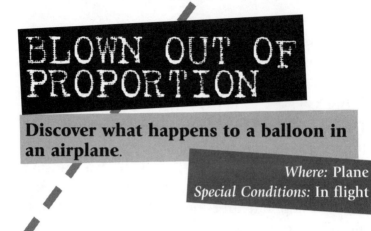

# BLOWN OUT OF PROPORTION

**Discover what happens to a balloon in an airplane.**

*Where:* Plane
*Special Conditions:* In flight

## Doing the Deed

The next time you go on an airplane, bring along a balloon, a piece of string, and a marker pen. While you're waiting for takeoff, blow up the balloon. Inflate it about halfway and knot the end. Wrap the string around the balloon. Make a mark on the string to indicate the diameter of the balloon. Also mark the balloon to show where the string was when you measured. You will need to measure in the same spot later.

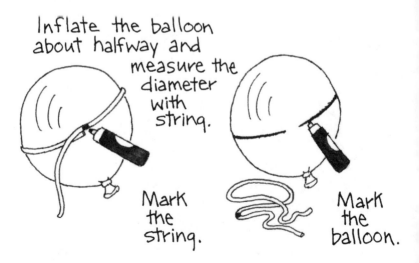

Inflate the balloon about halfway and measure the diameter with string.

Mark the string.

Mark the balloon.

When the plane has reached cruising altitude, measure the balloon again. You'll find that it has increased in size—just how much depends on the altitude at your takeoff location and the amount of pressurization in the cabin. The balloon will show what your ears have registered all along—the air pressure has definitely decreased.

As air pressure drops, the balloon expands.

## Insider Information

Air pressure is the weight of a column of air from the earth's surface to the end of the atmosphere. At sea level, a one-inch-square column weighs about fifteen pounds. As you go higher, there's less air above you, so it weighs less. It's also thinner, and there's less oxygen. An oxygen-starved flight is definitely a bad trip. To keep you comfortable, not to mention alive, airlines pressurize the cabin to about ten pounds per square inch, or two-thirds the pressure at sea level. It's as if you were at an altitude of about 6,000 feet. But that's still enough of a decrease to feel a difference.

Gases always obey the gas laws—anywhere, any time. One of them states that as the pressure on a gas decreases, its volume increases. In other words, as you go up and air pressure drops, the balloon expands. The reverse is also true. As you descend, the pressure increases and the volume decreases.

You can check out the differences with other things, such as your ears or a bottle of carbonated beverage. Notice how the cabin attendants are always careful when they open drinks filled with pressurized gas. As soon as the cap or pop top is loosened, the gas is free to expand. Its exit is sometimes quite dramatic as the soda rushes out in a fizzy explosion. To see the reverse effect, bring along an empty water bottle (one made from soft plastic). It should have a

COOL!

screw top. When you are up in the air, open the bottle, then shut it tightly again. When the plane has landed, you will have a collapsed container. Air pressure on the outside is now greater than that on the inside.

Why do your ears react to a change in air pressure? There is air on both sides of your eardrums. However, the air inside your head does not connect directly to the outside; it must go through tiny tubes. When the pressure on one side of your eardrum is greater than on the other, you feel pain. There are tricks that will help you equalize the pressure. On the way up, it's helpful to yawn. Caution! Yawning is contagious. On the way down, hold your nose, close your mouth, and blow very gently.

CAUTION! Blowing too hard may damage your ears.

# UPSCALE FLIGHT

**See your money increase as your plane takes off.**

*Where:* Plane
*Special Conditions:* During takeoff

## Doing the Deed

Watch your money carefully during takeoff. Coins get heavier as your plane climbs to its cruising altitude. The increase in weight is, unfortunately, only temporary. It is, however, measurable.

Bring a postage scale and some tape with you on a flight. Before takeoff, tape an ounce or more of coins on the scale—four quarters make about an ounce. The reason for the tape is to keep the coins from vibrating off the scale. Hold the scale on your armrest. Nothing will happen until the plane leaves the ground. As it climbs to its cruising altitude, watch the scale. You will see a small but noticeable increase in the weight of the coins.

## Insider Information

As the plane accelerates upward, it is working against gravity. There is an increased upward force that you feel as the seat cushion presses against you. The

tape — coins

Weight increases as airplane climbs.

arm rest

increased force also causes the scale to push harder against the coins. This is the same as saying that the coins are pushing down on the scale with increased pressure, which shows up as the weight gain. The weight gain occurs only when the plane is climbing. At a level altitude you will have lost your increased wealth. Easy come, easy go!

Some skyscrapers have high-speed elevators that will also "increase" your money. They have an advantage over an airplane as a testing area because you can see a weight loss as you go down. Planes descend too gradually for you to measure the loss with such an imperfect instrument as a postage scale.

# LAW-ABIDING BALLOON

**See how a balloon behaves differently in a car from the way you do.**

*Where:* Car, school bus
*Special Conditions:* En route

## Doing the Deed

Which should you trust: a balloon or your brain? Normally, we'd say, "Trust your brain." But sometimes a balloon is a better indicator of what's really happening.

Take a helium-filled balloon on a car ride. Sit in the rear seat and hold the string so that the balloon floats freely without touching anything. The balloon experiences a completely different trip from yours. When the car speeds up, you feel as if you are pressed against your seat back. The balloon, however, moves forward. If the car abruptly slows down, you feel yourself thrown forward. Only the seat belt saves you from going through the front windshield. The balloon, on the other hand, moves to the rear. When the car makes a right turn, you are thrown left, but the balloon goes right. A left turn, and the balloon moves the way the car moves. You tilt right.

# Insider Information

The balloon is observing the laws of physics. And in spite of the way it looks, so are you. When the car accelerates, everything that's not attached to the car resists the change in speed. That includes you, the air, and the balloon.

You are not easy to push around. Your weight resists the change in speed long enough for you to feel as if you're moving in the opposite direction. The air offers so little resistance that it accelerates at just about the same rate as the car. The helium-filled balloon, the lightest object in the car, is pushed forward by the speeding air. In fact, it actually goes slightly faster than the car. If the balloon were not on a string, it would keep going until it hit the windshield.

When the car maintains a constant speed, the string keeps the balloon in its original position. The force that displaces the balloon occurs only when the car is changing its speed or direction.

# FAKE LAKE

## See a mirage on the road.

*Where:* Car on highway
*Special Conditions:* Hot, sunny day

## Doing the Deed

Mirages are famous for luring thirsty desert travelers, who stagger toward an oasis only to discover that it doesn't exist. You don't have to be in a desert to see a fake lake. And you certainly don't have to be thirsty. The illusion of water in the distance can trick even a camera. This mirage has been photographed many times.

The best place to see a fake lake is on an asphalt road on a hot, sunny summer day. When you get to a place where the road is straight, look ahead for a patch of shimmering "water" in the distance. Oncoming cars can drive through this "desert car-wash" without making a splash. In fact, you can see a car's reflection in the fake lake. As you approach, the phantom puddle disappears, only to be replaced by another one farther down the road.

## Insider Information

Light bends when it travels from one transparent material to another. When you look at your feet in a

100

swimming pool, they are not where you expect them to be, because the image is bent when it passes from the water to the air. Hot air acts as if it were a different material from cooler air. Air rising over an asphalt roadbed is hotter than the air above it. Light from the sky bends at the boundary between the hot and cooler air. Instead of continuing in a straight path down to the road, it is bent toward your eyes. What you see is an image of the sky on the ground. Water reflects an image of the sky in the same manner. When you look at the mirage, your brain says, "I've seen this before. It's water." You can't tell the difference between a bent-light image of the sky and a similar image reflected from water.

Your brain isn't finished fooling you with this illusion. When there is a car in the distance, it sometimes appears to be traveling on a mirror. Because there are no waves and you see an undisturbed upside-down image of a car, you realize it can't be water. What can it be? Your brain, basing its interpretation on past experience, says it could be a mirror.

cool air

The image of the sky creates a mirage.

Hot air rises from the road.

6

# The Critter
# Connection

# BEWITCHING FROGS

## Become an expert in amphibian hypnosis with our four-minute course.

*Where:* Pond or pet store
*Special Conditions:* None

## Doing the Deed

You can be the master of a wild creature and put it in a trance. If you are new to casting spells, begin with a frog. In no way does this trick harm a frog, so a pet store may let you try it on one of their animals.

Pick up a frog in one hand. Turn it upside down. Gently stroke your finger up and down its belly. It may struggle for a few moments, but it will be unable to resist your magic touch. Continue stroking for a

few more seconds to put it into a very deep trance. At this point you can set it down and it will simply lie there, motionless, completely unaware of its surroundings. Frog trances last anywhere from a few minutes to an hour. *Be careful not to let the frog dry out, since it needs moist skin in order to breathe. If you turn out to be an especially gifted mesmerizer and your frog is entranced for more than fifteen minutes, sprinkle it with water.* The frog will come out of its trance naturally, or you can make it "come to" quickly by clapping your hands or gently prodding it with your finger. This is not a one-shot performance. You can repeat it over and over again on the same frog.

## Insider Information

Scientists don't know exactly why belly stroking hypnotizes some animals. But they believe that trances may be a form of protection. A lifeless-appearing prey is not as likely to trigger aggressive behavior from predators.

Just about every frog we've laid our hands on has fallen under our spell. We have not been as successful with toads. Some are hypnotizable; some are not.

Advanced charmers have also beguiled lizards, crocodiles, turkeys, chickens, ducks, rabbits, guinea pigs, mice, and snakes.

# BEE CALCULATING

## Honeybees can pass a test in higher mathematics with flying colors.

*Where:* Beehive
*Special Conditions:* Summertime

## Doing the Deed

Honeybees fly miles every day gathering nectar, the raw material of honey. When they find a good source, they fly back to the hive and communicate the location of the sweet stuff to other bees.

With a brain the size of the ball in a ballpoint pen, a honeybee figures how long a round trip from hive to flower will take, factoring in distance, wind resistance, and the weight of the nectar. You have to learn math, but bees are born with higher math skills. Here's an amazing test you can give the bees.

Dissolve as much sugar as you can in a half-cup of water. Put some of it in a dish and place it about 20 feet from a beehive. The bees will soon find the bait. The next day, move the dish 25 percent farther from the hive. It will now be 20 feet + 5 feet, or a total of 25 feet, from the hive. Refill the dish when the sugar water is gone. On the third day, move the dish 25 percent farther than it was on the second day. That is, 25 feet + 25 percent of 25, which is 6.25 feet, for a total of 31.25 feet. Each day place the plate 25 percent farther from the hive than it was on the previous day. Do this at approximately the same time every day for at least a week. After a few days, the bees will be waiting for you at the new location.

## Insider Information

The bees are doing a set of calculations known to mathematicians as a *geometric progression*. Figuring out a geometric progression requires more than simple addition or subtraction. A geometric progression is a sequence of numbers in which each number changes by the same percentage from the one before it. If you don't know how to do fractions or calculate percentages, you won't know where to position the plate.

No one has discovered how bees know what they know. Maybe you'll be the one to find out.

# A SWEET CHOICE

**See if ants can tell a diet drink from the real thing.**

*Where:* Outdoors anywhere
*Special Conditions:* When ants are active

## Doing the Deed

Manufacturers of diet soft drinks depend on fooling people. They are counting on the fact that drinks containing artificial sweeteners taste pretty much the same as those flavored with sugar. Ants don't seem to be as easily deceived as humans. Set up a taste test for ants, and see for yourself.

You'll need two cans of the same kind of soda, a diet one with aspartame (NutraSweet) and a sugar-sweetened one. Find an anthill. This shouldn't be too hard—ants are almost everywhere. Put a few drops of

each soft drink on a hard surface, such as a concrete walkway, a rock, or a patio stone near the anthill. There should be at least six inches between your two samples. Now wait. It won't be long before the first ant scouts discover your sweet temptations.

Ants definitely prefer the real thing. Within a few minutes, the word on the hill is that the sugared drink is the one to visit. Talk about effective advertising!

## Insider Information

The molecules of natural sugars fit into an ant's taste receptors, which are located on its antennae and in its mouth. Ants don't have receptors that fit aspartame molecules, so the artificial sweetener doesn't taste sweet to them. Since ants are not trying to lose weight, they correctly pass up the diet drink in favor of the one that will nourish them.

Ants, however, are not foolproof. They *can* be tricked by drinks sweetened with saccharin.

# ALARMING BREATH

**Your breath can frighten an entire community of ants.**

*Where:* Outdoors anywhere
*Special Conditions:* When ants are active

## Doing the Deed

You don't have to huff and puff on an anthill to get the ants' attention. Breathe gently on a single ant and the smell will terrorize her. In a short period of time, she will communicate her extreme panic to the rest of the colony. The other ants will charge to the rescue, searching frantically for the intruder with the unforgettable breath.

## Insider Information

The carbon dioxide in human breath is detected by receptors in an ant's antennae. The ant perceives this as a threat and responds with a typical ant alarm reaction. This consists of erratic movements and an odor of her own making that alerts the rest of the colony. Soldiers come to the strange-breath scene and fan out in search of the intruder, while other ants run around in panic. The soldiers are fully prepared to give up their lives in defense of their home.

However, if no more bad-breath attacks are launched in a minute or two, they will sound an all clear, and everyone will return to normal activities.

# HOT MUSIC

## Calculate the air temperature with a cricket.

*Where:* Outside
*Special Conditions:* Summer evenings

## Doing the Deed

On a warm summer night, you can use the sounds of crickets to figure out how hot it is. A digital watch or one with a second hand is the only tool you will need.

Count the number of cricket chirps you hear in fifteen seconds. Add 37 to the number you get. This is the temperature in degrees Fahrenheit. The frequency

Fifteen seconds!

I counted forty chirps.

40 + 37 = 77 degrees.

chirp! chirp!

of cricket chirping varies a little from species to species, but your calculation will be surprisingly accurate.

An assistant is helpful. Let one person concentrate on the counting while the other watches the watch.

## Insider Information

Crickets are living thermometers because, like most insects, they are more active when it is hot. Very few bugs have "voices." Most make sounds by scratching or rubbing their legs or wings. Crickets create their chirps by scraping the cover of their left wing across the rough edges of their right wing cover. The warmer it is, the more often they rub and the higher the pitch of the sound.

It's only the male crickets that fiddle away the night. Their song is a mating call designed to attract the silent females, who listen with ears located near their knees.

The music played at yard parties is not restricted to crickets' songs. Their relatives, grasshoppers and katydids, serenade too. Katydids make music the same way as crickets do. Grasshoppers, however, fiddle by rubbing their hind legs against their front wings. These songs can also be used to tell the temperature, but the math is complicated. (Use crickets. It's a lot easier.)

# FLIRTING WITH FIREFLIES

**Trick a firefly into seeking a flashlight as a mate.**

*Where:* Yard
*Special Conditions:* Summer evenings

## Doing the Deed

A firefly's flashing light is its language of love. Fireflies mate on summer nights. The female, who prefers not to fly, attracts a mate by flashing her light. A cruising male recognizes the signal from a female of his species and answers it. Seeing his response, the female flashes again. The male flies closer and closer, repeating his flirtatious flashes. The two-way conversation continues until the male lands near the female.

You, too, can flirt with a male firefly. In fact, it's a good way to catch one. Here's how to speak "firefly" with a penlight, a very small flashlight. Look for the light of a flying male. One of the most common species has a J-shaped flight path and flashes about every six seconds. The female of this species waits two seconds before flashing back.

When you see a flying male's light, count off two seconds (one chimpanzee, two chimpanzee) and then hold your flashlight near the ground and flash it for one second. Once you have attracted his attention, keep flashing like this and he will come right to you—maybe even land on your hand.

There are thousands of species of fireflies, more than two hundred in North America alone. Each one has a unique pattern of flashing and flying for each sex.

## Insider Information

First of all, fireflies are not really flies; they are beetles. Most of their life is spent as immature grubs (larvae). They live only two weeks as flashing adults, during which time their only mission is to find a mate. They produce a chemical reaction in their abdomens that releases energy in the form of a cold light. In fact, fire is another chemical reaction that produces light, but 80 percent or more of the energy released is heat, which would cook the creator if critters tried making light with fire. In contrast, 98 percent of the energy released by fireflies is light! And that's cool! While many other animals produce light, the firefly is the only one that blinks.

On very hot nights a firefly Romeo is in a little more of a hurry. Like other insects, fireflies are more active when the temperature increases. This is easy to see with a captured firefly. Catch one and put it in a glass jar with holes punched in the top. Time the seconds between flashes. Then place the jar in a bowl. Pour water that is warmer than the air into the bowl so that the water around the jar covers it halfway. Don't use water any hotter than you can put your hand into. If you do, you will get no flashes—just dead bugs.

When the air in the jar has had time to heat up, time the flashes again. A firefly flashes about every eight seconds on cool summer evenings and every four seconds on hot nights.

When you have finished studying your captive fire fly, be sure to release it.

Flashes every 8 seconds   Flashes every 4 seconds

# FIDDLING FOR WORMS

## A technique for attracting real creeps.

*Where:* Lawn or garden
*Special Conditions:* Nice weather

## Doing the Deed

Worms spend their days underground. At night they come out to munch on dirt and grass, which is why some people call them night crawlers. That's also why we say, "The early bird catches the worm." If you want to catch worms, you have to get up early—before they go back into their burrows.

There is, however, a way to get worms to come out during the day. It's called fiddling. A worm fiddle is made of two sticks, each about a foot-and-a-half long.

To make your worm fiddle, ask an adult to carve a point at the end of one stick. Then have him or her cut notches every few inches along the length of the other stick. Drive the pointed end of the first stick into the ground.

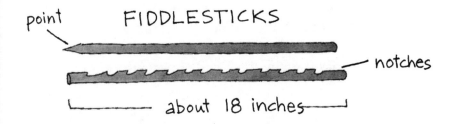

point    FIDDLESTICKS

notches

about 18 inches

Begin your worm serenade by drawing the notched stick like a violin bow across the stake in the ground. The bumping of the notches creates a rhythmic vibration below the ground. Continue your fiddling for five or six minutes. If you don't get results in ten minutes, move to another spot. The best places for a worm concert are lawns that are moist from a recent rain or watering.

## Insider Information

Worms don't have ears, but they sense danger when they feel vibrations. Most of the danger for a worm comes from above (remember the early bird), so surface vibrations cause them to seek the safety of their burrows. However, some dangers, such as moles, lurk in the soil. Worm fiddling sets up underground vibrations, tricking the worm into surfacing.

Charles Darwin, the noted nineteenth-century naturalist, had his own version of worm fiddling. He put a flowerpot with worms and soil on his piano. When he wanted to amuse guests, he played rhythmic bass notes on the piano. It was an odd tune, but the worms danced to it. Modernizing his parlor trick for the twentieth century, we used a rock-and-roll bass pattern on an electronic keyboard and got the same results from our wrigglers as Darwin got from his.

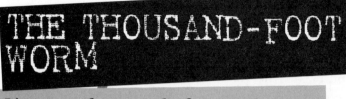

# THE THOUSAND-FOOT WORM

**Listen to the sound of an earthworm walking.**

*Where:* Yard
*Special Conditions:* Spring, summer, fall

## Doing the Deed

When you think about worms, you think wiggle, not walk. But they have hundreds of little footlike bristles called *setae* that propel them through the dirt.

You can hear an ordinary earthworm marching along if you place it on a piece of rough paper—very fine sandpaper is good. You will have to listen closely, of course, because the "feet" are very little. If you have trouble hearing the worm walking, roll a piece of paper into a cone and use it as a hearing aid. Put the small end near your ear and the wide end directly above the worm.

Another tip: If your worm is not very active, place

the paper in a well-lit spot, and the worm will start searching for shade.

## Insider Information

Not only can you hear the setae moving, you can feel them. Worms may be round, but they have a definite underside. Run your finger gently back and forth on a worm. The side that has the most resistance is the underside. Each segment has four pairs of setae. With a hand lens, you can see them. A full-grown earthworm has between 100 and 150 segments. That means almost a thousand marching "feet."

The worm uses the setae for traction as it pushes through the soil. When it is attacked, it digs them into tunnel walls and hangs on for dear life. You must be careful not to yank on a worm to get it out of the ground. It will break in half before it will let go.

An earthworm has no eyes, eats dirt, and breathes through its skin. That doesn't sound like an important critter. But think again. Without earthworms, the soil would be so compact that plants would die. It takes a whole lot of worms to be gardeners to the world. An acre of soil may contain more than a million of them. If all the worms were gathered up, they would weigh ten times the total weight of the entire human population. Or, put another way, that's 60 percent of the weight of all living animals on earth!

When you are finished listening to worms, remember to return them to the place where you found them. Don't just dump them on the lawn. They may have trouble finding their way back to their burrows.

# STRUGGLING MUSICIAN

Play music for a spider and see it come running.

*Where:* Yard
*Special Conditions:* None

## Doing the Deed

The original web surfer had to have been a spider. For millions of years spiders have been zooming around their wheel-like webs. You can get one of these eight-legged hunters to come scampering to you if you play music that sounds sweet to an arachnid.

To make the good vibrations, you need a tuning fork. (You can probably borrow one from the music room or from the science teacher.) A tuning fork that vibrates about 200 times a second is the perfect lure, although a fork that vibrates between 90 and 500 times a second will also work.

Grasp the fork by the handle and strike it against something solid, such as a piece of wood. Then hold one of the prongs of the humming fork against the web and watch. The spider will rush to the fork.

## Insider Information

A spider's web is a trap designed to catch flies and other insects. It's made of two types of silk. The circular strands are coated with an arachnid "glue," which holds insects that fly into it. The strands that form the spokes of the wheel are not sticky. They are the aerial highways on which the spider travels to its struggling prey so that it can deliver a fatal bite.

Once it has spun its web, the spider patiently waits in the center. When something becomes entangled, the spider identifies the struggler by the vibrations it sends along the strands. A fly's wings vibrate at about 200 times a second. And since a fly is a tasty treat for a spider, this frequency causes the spider to run down the web. Your tuning fork, vibrating at the same frequency as a buzzing fly, fools the spider.

Spiders are so tuned in to web vibrations they can even tell what kind of prey is trapped. You can see this by watching the way the spider approaches a struggling bug. A fly, which can't hurt the spider, brings the hungry hunter quickly and directly. When responding to a wasp, which is dangerous, the spider moves more slowly and cautiously so that it can zero in on the head and avoid being stung.

# 7

# Season Tickets

# LAWN GRAFFITI

## Express yourself in nonliving color by writing on your lawn with a garden hose.

*Where:* Lawn
*Special Conditions:* Not in winter

## Doing the Deed

A green lawn becomes a writing surface, and your garden hose becomes your writing tool. Arrange the hose to form a word in big looping script letters, or make a pattern or design. The message is limited only by the length of the hose. After twenty-four hours, peek under the hose. If the grass is pale green or yellow, remove the entire hose to expose your message in the grass. If the grass is still green, let the hose sit another day. Your message will appear in yellow letters against the green background of the lawn.

# Insider Information

You have just given your lawn a case of chlorosis. This disease is not fatal if you remove the hose in one or two days. Grass is green because of the green pigment *chlorophyll*. Without sunlight, the chlorophyll breaks down, leaving behind yellow blades of grass. But when the sunlight returns, the grass quickly recovers and makes new chlorophyll, and your message disappears. This is earth-friendly graffiti—it's self-erasing.

# EVERGREEN TOMATO

## Prevent a tomato from ripening, and fool the gardener.

*Where:* Vegetable garden
*Special Conditions:* Summer

## Doing the Deed

You are going to create a stubborn tomato. It will not turn red, and it will not ripen along with the other tomatoes on the plant. Although it still looks normal, our secret treatment will keep it evergreen.

Select a full-grown green tomato on a tomato plant. Being careful not to knock it off the plant, submerge the tomato in a container of very hot, but not boiling, water. Keep it covered with the water for three or four minutes. That's all there is to it. The tomato is not cooked, but the heat has stopped the ripening process cold.

1. Select a green tomato.
hot water

hot water
2. Submerge it for 3 or 4 minutes.

# Insider Information

Like many fruits, tomatoes produce ethylene gas, which causes them to ripen. The hot-water treatment damages the enzyme that produces the ethylene gas. But it doesn't kill the tomato. You can prove this by planting some of the seeds from your treated tomato. They'll grow, whereas the seeds from a cooked tomato won't grow.

Tomatoes don't have to produce their own ethylene gas in order to ripen. Ethylene gas from an outside source will work just as well. Commercial tomato growers often pick green tomatoes and pipe ethylene gas into the storage area.

Will your heat-treated tomato ripen if it receives a shot of ethylene gas? Test this by putting the evergreen tomato in a plastic bag with a ripe banana, an excellent source of ethylene gas. Commercially "gassed" tomatoes normally take three to four days to ripen.

A tomato expert told us that the science of ripening is not completely understood. But clearly, this experiment proves that the ripening process is blocked by heat. Not only can't the heated tomato produce ethylene gas, but it can't respond to it either.

3. Evergreen!

**Develop a picture of yourself on an apple.**

*Where:* Orchard
*Special Conditions:* Late summer

## Doing the Deed

Find a negative of a photograph that you can sacrifice in the name of science. It can be either a black-and-white or a color negative. Both will come out red and green in apple fruitography.

You will need:

> green apple on a tree
> light-proof bag
> negative
> egg white
> scissors
> tape

Select a full-sized but still-green apple on a tree. Don't pick it! While it's still on the tree, enclose it in a light-proof bag, such as a foil-lined bag used for take-out chicken. Leave the bag on the apple for a week. This will make the apple particularly light-sensitive. At the end of the week, remove the bag and

1. Don't pick it.

2. Put a bag on the apple for a week.

3. Glue a negative to the apple with egg white.

4. Cut a hole in the bag the size and shape of the negative.

5. Rebag the apple, taping so the negative shows through the hole. Develop for one week.

6. A fruitograph!

glue your negative onto the apple with beaten egg white. Cut a hole in the bag the size and shape of the negative. Put the bag back on the apple, taping it so that the negative shows through the hole. Give it another week to develop. When you take off the bag and the negative, your image will appear in red on a pale green background.

## Insider Information

During the ripening process, fruit becomes softer, sweeter, and tastier, and it changes color to advertise its deliciousness. Light plays a role in the development of the red pigment, called *anthocyanin*, in an apple. The transparent parts of the negative let light through and the color develops. The dark parts of the negative keep the apple skin from receiving light and developing. Fruitography doesn't work on Granny Smith or Golden Delicious apples. There's not enough color change in those varieties to make a print.

We've heard that some fruitographers use tomatoes, eggplants, pumpkins, and squash for their portraits. Perhaps you could think of someone to print on next year's Halloween pumpkin!

# SNOW JOB

## Create a snowy tempest from a teacup.

*Where:* Yard
*Special Conditions:* Very cold, dry winter day

## Doing the Deed

> CAUTION! This activity requires boiling water, so get an adult assistant to help you.

Have your adult assistant carry a cup of very hot water outside on an extremely cold, dry day—near 0° Fahrenheit (-18° Celsius) or below. Tell him or her to throw the water, not the cup, up into the air. *Aim it away from the two of you, other people, and pets.* Watch carefully. The water will turn into snow and fall to the ground.

## Insider Information

Snow forms when tiny drops of water freeze in the

air. In order for water to change from a liquid drop into a solid crystal, it must lose heat energy. There are several factors that affect snow formation:

- *Droplet size*—The smaller the droplet, the faster the freezing.
- *Air temperature*—The colder the air, the faster the freezing.
- *Humidity*—The drier the air, the faster water evaporates. Because evaporation has a cooling effect, it speeds up freezing.
- *Droplet temperature*—The hotter the water, the faster the water molecules at the surface of a droplet evaporate. This creates an enhanced cooling effect on the surface of the droplet, making it freeze more quickly.
- *Water purity*—Since ice crystals form around foreign particles, the more impurities there are in the water, the more ice crystals there will be. If there are no impurities, water can be cooled to -40° Fahrenheit (-40° Celsius) without ice crystals forming.

When the water is thrown into the air, it has to freeze before it hits the ground in order to make snow. It doesn't have a lot of time. To increase its chances, choose a very cold, dry day. Have your adult assistant throw the water as high as possible; this gives the droplets more time to form an ice shell. Use hot water to enhance the cooling effect of evaporation; this makes the ice shell form more quickly. Don't use distilled water; tap water has the necessary impurities to form centers around which ice can form.

Man-made snow is big business. Ski resorts rely on it when nature fails. Snow making was discovered in Florida in the 1950s when some farmers were spraying crops with water to keep them from freezing. They sprayed too fine a mist and got snow. This surprise gave birth to a new industry. Today, snow guns spraying water under pressure can create enough snow to cover a mountain of ski trails.

# FAST-FROZEN BUBBLES

**Soap bubbles take on a few new wrinkles when you blow them in frigid weather.**

*Where:* Yard
*Special Conditions:* A very cold winter day

## Doing the Deed

You might think that blowing bubbles is a summer activity. It is—but it can be a whole new experience in the dead of winter. Wait for an exceptionally cold day: 10° Fahrenheit (-12° Celsius) or below. Create bubbles with ordinary bubble solution and a wand. You should see some pretty amazing results.

First try drawing the wand through the air. Then try blowing on it.

At first, all you've got are normal bubbles, and some of them break right away. But some live long enough to freeze. Their perfect surfaces develop wrinkles, and then they break. Fragments of frozen bubbles don't disappear into the air. Pieces of the frozen soap film, which look like broken eggshells, fall to earth.

## Insider Information

A bubble's skin is like a sandwich—there is a layer of water molecules between two layers of soap molecules. Temperatures of 10° Fahrenheit and lower are well below the freezing point of water. This is cold enough to ensure that the thin layer of water in the bubble will freeze quickly, before the bubble has the chance to burst.

The bubbles formed by drawing a wand through the air freeze almost instantly. The bubbles blown by your mouth contain warm air. When they hit the cold outside air, the air inside the bubble contracts as it cools, causing the skin to crinkle like plastic wrap. The soap film adds strength to the frozen wall of the bubble.

When an unfrozen bubble bursts, the liquid soap film forms tiny drops as soon as the air escapes. The soap film in a frozen bubble is solid and it stays that way even if it's broken into pieces.

# SNOW FAKE

**Create the illusion of snow on a summer night.**

*Where:* By the side of a road, yard
*Special Conditions:* Summer night

## Doing the Deed

Sometimes you can see trees glistening in the moonlight as if they were covered with snow—in August! The summer "snow" has been seen mostly by night drivers whose headlights strike dew-coated branches of certain trees. The dew appears white. Since dew lands on the tops of branches, where snow also falls, the tree looks snow-laden. It is possible to see this illusion only under special conditions. Although the right circumstances do not occur very often in nature, don't worry—they're easy to set up.

Do this well after sundown, when it is very dark outside. Armed with a flashlight and a spray bottle filled with water, search for a plant with a waxy coating on its leaves. Shrubs and trees that make good snow fakes include blue spruce, juniper, cedar, hemlock, and rhododendron.

Spray water from your bottle on the waxy leaves. Then step back and shine your light on the wet area. Ta-da! Summer snow!

# Insider Information

This is an optical effect very similar in principle to the light-reflecting license plates that you investigated in Spy License on page 14. You may recall that the coating on the license plates is made of tiny glass beads with a mirror backing. In Snow Fake, your lenses are not glass beads but water droplets. And instead of a mirror backing, a thin layer of air between the water bead and the leaf creates the reflecting surface. Scientists call this reflection *sylvanshine*.

Leaves with a thick coating of microscopic waxy rods called a *bloom* make water bead up into almost perfect spheres. These spheres act as tiny lenses and channel light directly back at the observer.

If you find a hedge with good sylvanshine, you can spray an environmentally friendly message that can be read by drivers whose headlights strike the hedge.

**Discover the built-in springs of a dandelion.**

*Where:* Yard, fields
*Special Conditions:* Spring

## Doing the Deed

You probably don't think of plants as being especially quick. But dandelion stems can spring into action with amazing speed.

Among the first flowers you spot in the springtime are dandelions. Find a yellow dandelion blossom and pick it. With your fingernail, slit the stem lengthwise into four strips.

Put the dandelion into a glass of water. Watch the stem. In a matter of seconds, it begins to move. Each section of the stem rolls into a tight curl.

## Insider Information

Dandelions are members of a group of plants called *stem succulents.* They store water in cells located on the inside of the stem, and the water-filled cells become a column strong enough to support the flower. This property has survival value for plants. Succulent cells can store water for a long period of time, enabling the plant to survive droughts. When rain comes, the inside cells suck up water rapidly. This is what is happening when you put your slit-stem dandelion into water. Those interior cells swell up with as much water as they can hold, expanding in size. But now the cells on the inside of the stem are longer than the outer stem cells. And when one side of something is longer than the other, you get curls.

This phenomenon puts new meaning into the phrase "spring flowers."

# PLANT THERMOMETER

**Use a rhododendron bush to tell the temperature.**

*Where:* Yard, park
*Special Conditions:* Winter

## Doing the Deed

The American rhododendron, one of the most common yard plants, has such a curious response to cold that you can use it as a thermometer.

In mild weather (40–50° Fahrenheit, or 4–10° Celsius), the leaves of the rhododendron are bright green and perfectly flat. Around freezing (32° Fahrenheit, or 0° Celsius), the leaves darken in color and start to droop, and the edges begin to curl under. When the mercury drops to 0° Fahrenheit (-18° Celsius), the leaves turn almost black, hang down, and roll up tightly.

So, to see what kind of coat you will need on a winter morning, check a rhododendron.

## Insider Information

The strange behavior of rhododendron leaves has been the subject of intense scientific study, and there have been many theories about why the leaves of this

50° F          32° F          0°F

broadleaf evergreen darken and curl. The most recent explanation of the phenomenon is that bright sunlight and very cold temperatures permanently damage the cells of rhododendron leaves. By curling up and drooping its leaves, the plant reduces the amount of leaf surface exposed to the elements. Support for this explanation comes from the observation that when the leaves are covered with snow, they don't curl up.

Scientists have also found that frozen leaves are also damaged if they thaw too rapidly. Curled leaves thaw more slowly.

The rhododendron has clearly mastered some cold-weather survival strategies.

# APPLE FLINGSHOT

## Throw a green apple the length of a football field.

*Where:* A field near an apple tree
*Special Conditions:* Summer

## Doing the Deed

A flingshot is sort of like a slingshot. With it, you can throw an apple a lot farther than you can with your arm alone. Where can you get such a powerful missile launcher? No problem. A flingshot is just a thin flexible stick about three feet long that will spring back when you whip it through the air.

CAUTION! Before you launch any green missiles, make sure that you are in an open field. Don't aim at people, animals, or property that could be injured or damaged.

There are always green apples under an apple tree in the summer. Ask permission to use the "drops." If it's okay, impale one on the end of your flingshot. But be careful! You are now in possession of a potentially dangerous plaything.

When you've cleared your apple for takeoff, grasp the end of the stick. Hold the flingshot so the apple is touching the ground in front of you. In one motion, bend your elbow and swing the apple back over your shoulder and then quickly bring your arm forward in a whipping motion. At the fullest extension of your arm, flick your wrist as your arm comes to an abrupt stop. The apple will rocket off in the direction your arm is pointing. As in other sports, flingshot skills improve with practice.

## Insider Information

The ideal quarterback would have arms that hung to the ground. Extra length multiplies the speed and the distance of a thrown object. The flingshot is an arm extender, a kind of lever that increases the speed of the apple. The faster the apple moves, the greater the distance it will travel before it hits the ground. The little flick of the wrist that you give when you stop your arm is to shake the apple loose.

The texture of a green apple is absolutely perfect for this sport. Other fruits and vegetables can be launched, but we haven't found any that rival an apple for distance. Maybe you'll discover a record-setting veggie or flying fruit.

# 8

# The Explorer's Club

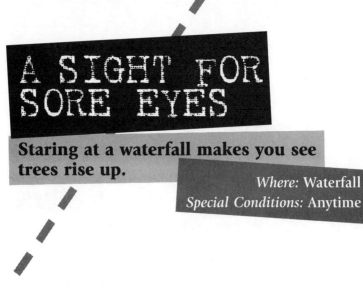

# A SIGHT FOR SORE EYES

**Staring at a waterfall makes you see trees rise up.**

*Where:* Waterfall
*Special Conditions:* Anytime

## Doing the Deed

First, find a waterfall. After you've admired the beauty of this natural phenomenon, create another one with your own eyes. Stare at the waterfall for about thirty seconds. Then shift your gaze to the nearby trees on a bank next to the falls. The trees will appear to move upward. This illusion is not limited to trees. You can even move mountains.

## Insider Information

In your eyes there are pairs of receptors that track motion. Receptors for downward motion are paired with receptors for upward motion. When you look at a waterfall, the downward-motion receptors are fired. Stare long enough and these receptors get tired. When you shift your gaze to a stationary object, these tired downward-motion receptors no longer fire. Strange but true, when one member of paired receptors is not firing, the other is activated, even though

148

nothing is moving. In this case, the upward-motion receptors are free to fire, and you perceive motion when there is none.

If you're a city kid, you can still have this uplifting experience by looking at artificial waterfalls or fountains.

You can also try this from inside your own personal waterfall—the shower. Gaze at the falling drops, and then watch the rising tide in your soap dish.

# GOO TO GO

## Use the sticky goo from a pine tree to propel sticks across a pond.

*Where:* Woods and water
*Special Conditions:* Spring, summer, fall

## Doing the Deed

Pines and other evergreen trees produce a thick, sticky material called *resin*. To build an amazing racing boat, you'll need to collect a big blob of this resin. Check out nearby pine trees, and see if one has had a recent injury. If it has, you'll find dried, whitish gum on the trunk. This is the resin that you need. If you can't find an injured tree, pull off a small branch, at the spot where it attaches to the trunk. Soon goo will ooze out of the wound. Take a small stick and collect a gob of goo on the end of it. (Be careful not to get any on your clothes or skin. It's hard to remove without using turpentine.) This goo stick is your racer, and it is now all fueled up and ready to go.

Find a large puddle or pond, and place the stick in the water with the gooey end nearest the shore. The resin racer will shoot forward, without a push from you, sailing across the water at a steady pace.

If you have a friend with you, launch a resin-powered boat race.

# Insider Information

The stick moves, but the propellant is not really the resin. It's the water itself. The molecules on the water's surface cling together like a skin. The force holding water molecules together at the surface is called the *surface tension*. Pine resin forms a film on the water, breaking surface tension for an instant. The water's surface repairs itself, creating a turbulence that pushes the stick forward. This is the same kind of disturbance you can see in the experiment called Troubled Waters on page 50. The rubbing alcohol in Troubled Waters eventually dissolves in the water, but resin does not, so the process is repeated over and over. This series of little pushes moves your boat steadily toward the finish line.

**Stage one of the world's slowest races with mysterious creeping blobs.**

*Where:* Woods
*Special Conditions:* Not winter

## Doing the Deed

When people first saw slime molds, they thought they were aliens from outer space. But these unidentified growing objects turned out to be a remarkable living thing. For a long time scientists didn't know how to classify them. But they were so entertaining that some people kept them as pets. They even held slime mold races.

If you'd like to try, collect some slime mold from the woods. The best places to find slime molds are inside rotting logs and under the leaf litter on the forest floor. Look for a blob of yellowish goo that may have veins in it like a leaf. (There's little doubt why "slime" is its first name.) Pick it up in a plastic bag or small container. Don't worry about being slimed. It's disgusting-looking but harmless.

The race course can be a dinner plate. Put two or more small blobs of slime mold on one side of the plate. At the finish line, the other side of the plate, put some pieces of dry oatmeal, which is one of their

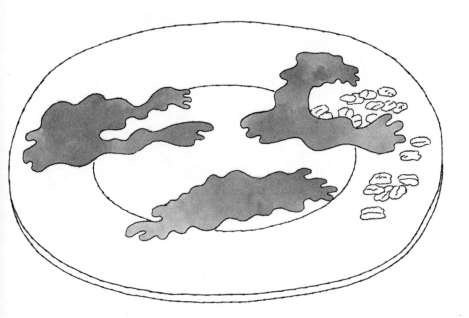

favorite foods. With a speed approaching that of a snail, your slimy competitors will creep toward their reward. The pulsating slime mold engulfs the oatmeal like a giant amoeba.

## Insider Information

Slime molds are truly weird. For openers, they have eighteen different sexes. They are not plants. They're not animals. And they're not fungi. But at different times during their bizarre life cycle, they have characteristics of each of these groups. Scientists finally decided that they belonged in a separate kingdom called *Protoctista*.

Slime molds are still very much a mystery. But they sure are fun to play with.

# SLUDGE BUSTERS

## Clean up an oil spill by souping up nature's sanitation squad.

*Where:* Yard, beach, vacant lot
*Special Conditions:* Not winter

## Doing the Deed

An oil tanker on the rocks is not the only source of environmental contamination. Every day millions of cars, especially old ones, drip oil on roads and driveways. Rain washes these pollutants into the surrounding soil. If you look around your neighborhood, you will probably find a small unsightly oil spill that is polluting the soil. This is your golden opportunity to help clean up the environment!

Get some liquid plant fertilizer—one that contains nitrogen. If the polluted soil is hard-packed, break it up with garden tools so air can get into it. Spray or sprinkle the fertilizer on the sludge until the soil is dampened. *Be sure to wash your hands after you work around oil spills.*

It takes only a minute or two to pollute the environment, but it's going to take longer to clean it up. You should start to see a difference after two weeks. If all the oil isn't gone, repeat the fertilizer treatment.

# Insider Information

A spoonful of soil has been estimated to contain 5 billion bacteria. Some of these happen to like oil as food. At nature's pace, it would take decades for them to eat your oil spill. If you can encourage their appetites, however, they will eat faster and clean up an oil spill quickly. The nitrogen in fertilizer stimulates the appetite of the sludge busters, so they eat more. They digest the gooey oil, producing nonpolluting carbon dioxide and water as waste products.

Using microorganisms to restore natural environmental conditions is called *bioremediation*. The first time it was used on a large scale was after the huge 1989 *Exxon Valdez* oil spill in Alaska. Of all the methods used to try to clean the beaches, the most effective one was spraying them with ordinary farm fertilizer. Two weeks after treatment, scientists observed the area from a helicopter. Much to their surprise, the fertilized beaches looked clean.

Of course, not all soil bacteria have a taste for oil. There are specialists that thrive on a strict diet of petroleum. Bioremediation companies sell packages of oil eaters. They also sell bacteria to eat radioactive waste, sewage, and garbage. They have discovered microbes that can clean up over 90 percent of all hazardous chemical substances. The new science of bioremediation gets the job done better, faster, and cheaper.

# FLYING SAUCER

## Send a paper plate racing up a kite string.

*Where:* Beach, wide open spaces
*Special Conditions:* Windy day

## Doing the Deed

Go fly a kite! It's fun. You can make it even more of an adventure with a line traveler. Use a paper plate and you've got a genuine flying saucer.

Aside from the paper plate, you will need a pair of scissors and some tape. Unless you can tie your kite to something while you prepare for the launch, you had better enlist the help of an assistant.

Using the points of the scissors, make a small hole (a little bit bigger than the diameter of the kite string) in the exact center of the plate. Cut a slit from the edge of the plate to the hole. Slide the plate onto the kite string with the bottom of the plate facing the

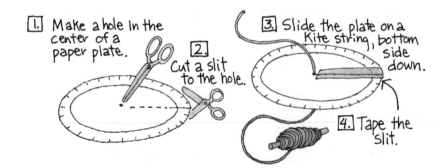

1. Make a hole in the center of a paper plate.

2. Cut a slit to the hole.

3. Slide the plate on a kite string, bottom side down.

4. Tape the slit.

ground. Tape the slit closed. Make sure the plate slides easily on the string.

Once you get the kite aloft, push the plate up the kite string until the plate catches the wind. It will travel up the string till it hits the kite. Sometimes the plate stops rising if it blows against the string. But when the wind shifts, your flying saucer will continue climbing.

## Insider Information

Line travelers, or kite ferries, as some people call them, are as old as kite flying, which is an ancient sport. Over the years, kite fliers have invented some very clever variations. Sometimes they put a stop, such as a cork, partway up the string. One kind of traveler releases a parachute when it hits the stop. Another has a trigger mechanism that collapses a sail and sends the kite ferry back down the line.

Kite shops sell travelers in many different styles, including airplanes and butterflies. We think it's more fun to invent your own.

One of the best things about a paper-plate traveler is the puzzled look of passersby as they try to iden-tify your very identifiable flying object. It is easier to believe in a flying saucer than a flying paper plate.

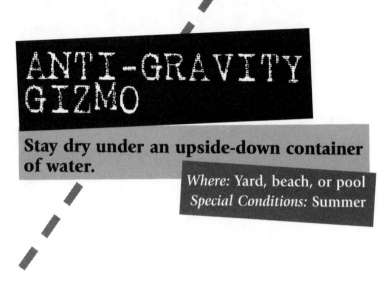

# ANTI-GRAVITY GIZMO

**Stay dry under an upside-down container of water.**

*Where:* Yard, beach, or pool
*Special Conditions:* Summer

## Doing the Deed

You can't say there are no strings attached to this trick. Strings help you create a force greater than gravity. Take a quart-sized disposable plastic container and make three evenly spaced holes near the rim. Cut three 2-foot lengths of string. Slip a piece of strong string through each hole and tie it securely. Knot the loose ends of the three strings together. This is your anti-gravity gizmo. Fill it half full of water.

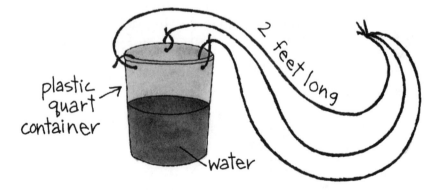

plastic quart container

2 feet long

water

Swing the coverless container back and forth like a pendulum, building up speed and the length of the swing. Your goal is to make a complete circle. The container will be upside-down some of the time, but the water will not fall out. Keep it moving and stay confidently dry.

CAUTION! Before you start swinging, make sure no one is standing too close to you.

## Insider Information

There are two forces acting on the container. First, you exert a force to move the container away from you in a straight line. Second, the strings exert a force to prevent this from happening and to pull the container toward your hand. The result of these two forces is that the container makes a circular path at the end of the strings.

The combination produces a centrifugal, or away-from-the-center, force on the water inside the container, pressing it against the bottom. When the container is upside-down, you have obviously created an anti-gravity force that is stronger than gravity.

159

# GRAVEYARD BEACH?

**Test a beach and discover where it came from.**

*Where:* Beach
*Special Conditions:* None

## Doing the Deed

It takes millions of years to make a beach. Those tiny grains of sand were once something else. Some are minerals that were originally part of larger rocks. Some are minerals that used to be part of living things. Some are even from outer space. (Check it out in the Cosmic Sand activity on page 166.) Some beaches have sand from only one source, while others contain sand from a variety of sources.

One of the most common kinds of sand is made of limestone, known to scientists as calcium carbonate. The sources of limestone are shells and skeletons of marine life. If you want to know whether you are walking on the remains of dearly departed sea critters, test for limestone. To detect the limestone, you'll need distilled white vinegar and a paper cup or some other kind of small container. Put some sand in the bottom of the container. Pour in enough vinegar to cover the sand. Watch for bubbles. If they appear, you know that your beach is a graveyard.

# Insider Information

This test takes advantage of the fact that calcium carbonate reacts with acids. Vinegar is an acid—although a very weak one. However, it is powerful enough to react with limestone. When it does, carbon dioxide gas bubbles to the surface. Other kinds of sand don't react this way, so this is the acid test for limestone!

In nature, slightly acidic water dissolves limestone. Sometimes these limestone-water solutions drip into caves and the water evaporates, leaving behind stalagmites and stalactites made of calcium carbonate.

# KNEAD A BALLOON?

**Sand becomes an amazing plastic material inside a balloon.**

*Where:* Beach
*Special Conditions:* None

## Doing the Deed

Make a sandbag. This is most easily done with a balloon. Take a funnel or a piece of paper rolled up like a funnel and stick it into the neck of the balloon. Pour in enough sand to almost fill the balloon. If the sand stops running into the balloon before the balloon is filled, squeeze the balloon to let out air. Knead the balloon a few times to get the feel of the dry sand.

Now, pour enough water into the balloon to cover the sand. Again, you may have to release air. Tie a knot in the end of the balloon. Squeeze the balloon

1. Fill the balloon with sand.

2. Add water to cover the sand.

a few times. The sand doesn't feel the same as it did before, does it? It is a plastic material now that is fun to knead.

*Note:* If you don't have a balloon, you can try this with a plastic bag.

## Insider Information

A mound of sand is made up of tiny rock crystals that are piled on top of one another in no real order. The spaces between the grains are filled with air. When you pour water over the grains, the water flows around the grains, replacing the air. But water does what air can't. It lubricates the sand crystals. This allows the grains to move closer together and become densely packed.

Wet sand is a plastic—a material that is easily molded. Knead your sandbag, and see all the shapes you can make. As every sandcastle builder knows, wet sand holds its shape even without a balloon.

A substance that allows a nonplastic to become a plastic is called a *plasticizer.* In this case, water is the plasticizer. Do you think another lubricant, such as salad oil, can do the same job? Experiment and find out.

3. Tie a Knot.    4. Shape it!

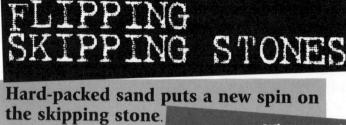

# FLIPPING SKIPPING STONES

**Hard-packed sand puts a new spin on the skipping stone.**

*Where:* Beach
*Special Conditions:* Low tide

## Doing the Deed

Almost everyone has skipped stones across water. The best stones for throwing are oval flat ones about two or three inches long. The best throwing motion is a sidearm one, snapping the wrist just before the release. The idea is to put a spin on the stone as it flies off roughly parallel to the water. In a good throw, the stone skips or hops repeatedly along the surface of the water. The world record is twenty-four hops. But records, of course, can be broken. Go for it!

If the water is rough when you're at the beach, try skipping stones on the sand. Near the water's edge, the sand is wet and hard packed. This is the perfect surface for the land version of this sport. Skip a stone there exactly as you would on water.

You'll notice that stones skip differently on sand. On water, the first hop is the longest; the others get progressively shorter. On sand, the first hop is short, followed by a much longer hop similar to the first hop on the water. Additional hops alternate between short and long. The evidence of this unusual pattern is marked in the sand.

## Insider Information

Friction causes the stone to flip over when it hits the sand, so the short hop is not a skip, it's a flip. Friction is a force between two surfaces moving against each other. It slows down motion. There's not as much friction on water, so the stone doesn't flip. Instead, the back edge builds a wave in front of it, which gives added lift to its flight. As a result, you'll get a lot more skips on water.

# COSMIC SAND

## Find meteorites at the beach.

*Where:* Beach
*Special Conditions:* None

## Doing the Deed

Meteors, or shooting stars, are rocks from space that burn when they enter the earth's atmosphere. If they are not completely vaporized, as most are, and if they survive to land on the surface of the earth, they are called *meteorites*. Finding a large meteorite is very difficult because they are extremely rare. But you can find tiny ones, because meteorites are constantly falling onto the earth's surface. They are everywhere, but the easiest place to collect them is at the beach.

Your high-tech meteorite collection kit consists of a magnet inside a plastic bag. Drag it through the sand. The tiny particles will stick to the magnet through the bag. To collect them, carefully turn the bag inside out so that the particles are trapped in the bag. Remove the magnet and shake the particles into another plastic bag. Continue "mining" the beach until you have as many space rocks as you want. Congratulations! You now own some extraordinarily ancient stuff. Your sand may be 4.6 billion years old. That's a billion years older than any earth rock.

## Insider Information

The reason that you use a magnet to collect meteorites is that meteorites are mostly iron. And, as you probably know, iron is attracted to magnets. All of the material you collected is not necessarily from outer space. Scientists have estimated, however, that about 20 percent of the magnetic material on the earth's surface is from other places in the cosmos. If you want to make sure that you have collected some cosmic sand, look at it with a strong magnifying lens

or, better yet, under a microscope. Meteorite particles are nearly perfect spheres, although in time some of them may be worn down by erosion and become irregular in shape.

Why are meteorites usually round? When meteorites enter the earth's atmosphere, air resistance causes them to heat up just like a reentering spaceship. The iron becomes red-hot and melts. Liquids become spheres when they are falling freely. (Falling raindrops are spheres, not teardrop-shaped.) By the time the meteorite particles hit the ground, they have cooled and hardened in their spherical shape.

If you're not near a beach, you can still collect cosmic sand. The roof of a house is a large surface area, and a lot of meteorite dust lands on it. When it rains, the dust is washed into the rain gutters. If you place a plastic-bag-covered magnet in the stream of water that gushes out of the downspout, the magnetic dust will cling to it. The best time to collect the dust is as soon as water starts to flow from the roof after several days of dry weather.

# Index of Places

amusement parks, 56

beaches, 154, 156, 158, 160, 162, 164, 166
beehives, near, 106

cars, 84, 98, 100
classrooms, 36, 44, 46, 50, 52
computer labs, 39

decks, 25
driveways, 14, 60

fields, 140, 144

gardens, 117, 128, 132
gyms, 42, 44, 48

lawns, 117, 126
libraries, 80

orchards, 130, 144

parking lots, 14
parks, 142, 156. *See also* yards
patios, 25, 60. *See also* yards
pet stores, 104
planes, 58, 86, 88, 90, 92, 96
playgrounds, 60, 62, 64, 66, 84
ponds, 104, 150, 158

restaurants, 70, 72, 74
roadside, 138

# Index